# I WAS GOD FOR
# A SECOND

## 50 ESSAYS

## By
## Mo Pulido

Published by: Author's Hike

ISBN: E-book: 978-1-964687-41-4

Paperback: 978-1-964687-42-1

Hardcover: 978-1-964687-09-4

Printed in: United States of America

First Edition: May, 2024

Cover design by: Author's Hike

Interior design by: Author's Hike

Some people walk around in a dream, as it were; they are the dreamers who, childlike, walk around in a pure dream and radiate purity, infecting or purifying everyone around them.

# Table of Contents

# 1

## God and I Are Pretty Much Brothers

I have everything to say about everything. It's not an exaggeration to say I can say everything about what's going on in this world and in the next world, the afterlife, if that's what you want to call it. I call it just a continuation of this life; there's no difference between now and later. It's all a continuum. Why say life is better than death? It's not. It's just two states of the same existence–none better than the other, life equal to death, death equal to the next incarnation. Not that I believe in reincarnation, but something will happen to our bodies and souls after we die. They don't just disappear. It could be millennia, but we all will take another form. It could be billions of years from now. I don't mind waiting that long. Most people don't want to wait that long, so they say we'll be resurrected, reincarnated, or other such nonsense. Can't blame people for dreaming. They want to be resurrected in three days, but it's not going to happen, it never did happen, except in some fantasy. Nothing wrong with fantasies, but let's get real. Let's just say we all get resurrected, or our cells get reborn in some form or another, in, say, ten billion years from now. I'm okay with that. I can wait that long. No problem. The later, the better because good things take a long time, and the less we're like our current incarnation, the better. We didn't turn out so great this time–sure, beautiful for a few minutes, perfect for a few minutes, but that didn't last long. Even as we were growing, we were dying spiritually. That's a fact. We were pure at

1

birth, but it was all downhill after that. Not our fault the material world is imperfect, but maybe next time, we can be incarnated into something better, longer lasting. Not that I want to live forever. I don't. I just want to live long enough to see God.

I saw God the day I was born but haven't seen Him since, though I wanted to. I wanted to see Him daily, but you can't see God unless you're pure enough to be in His presence. I was that pure on day one, but not afterward. It wasn't my fault, but that's mortality for you. It corrupts your soul, whether you like it or not. The point is I want to live long enough in my next incarnation to see God again. I can do it if I live long enough. If I have the time to purify my soul again, as it were, which pretty much takes a million years. So, I have to live that long if I want to see God again. I do. I want to see Him because He and I are pretty much brothers. You see, we're like twins, God and I, both born simultaneously. Only one becomes God, and the other becomes just a mortal, fallible human being. None better than the other, but one becomes a deity, and the other becomes either a saint, criminal, or something in between. Nothing wrong with that, but either way, you can't see God again. You're too impure. You can't see your own brother again until you're pure enough, even if it takes a million or a billion years or ten billion years. I can wait that long to see God, my brother, my flesh and blood. We were born at the same time. He went His way, and I went mine. We can't see each other again until I purify myself, as pure as I was when I was born alongside Him. See, God was born at the same time I was born. We're twins, brothers, kin. I could have been God, and He could have been a mortal soul. It doesn't really matter whether He turned out to be God or I did. It could have happened either way. I don't mind being a mortal soul. Don't mind being impure as all hell. It's just that I can't see my brother again until I purify myself. It could take a billion or a trillion years. It doesn't matter. I can wait that long. I don't mind waiting. I just want to see my brother again sometime. It doesn't matter when. We'll be reunited. And at that point, He might say, "Why don't you be God for now, for a trillion years or so? I'm tired of being God. There's too much pressure, too many expectations, demands. So why don't you be God for a trillion trillion years, and I'll be mortal? I don't mind. One is as good as the other. You're as good as me right now, even though I'm God and you're not. So, let's swap places. You be God, and I'll be a man. One is as good as the other. I should know; I'm God. Or now I'm man, and now you're God. We just switched. Now you're God. You deal with it. You'll find that it's just the same as being a man, neither better than the other, neither all that—in fact, I'd say it's better to be a man than God. At least there's not all that pressure to be perfect. I don't want to be perfect. I want to have a good time. You can't have a good time if you're perfect, if you're God. I'd rather be man, now that I'm man, even though I only live a little while. I don't mind. I don't mind being just a mortal, imperfect man because I know, deep down, that I'm God also. Born of the flesh, I'm man, but I'm also God. All of us humans are."

# 2

## Better to Be Wrong Than Right

I do whatever I want. That's who I am. I'm a free spirit; this is my world. It belongs to me, the whole wide world and everything in it. It all belongs to me, and more importantly, I belong to the world. I wouldn't exist without it; it wouldn't exist without me. I mean, I made the world. Before the universe, there was nothing. I made it; I brought it into existence. Who am I to say that? Am I some kind of God, or am I actually God Himself or Herself? It doesn't matter who I am.

People make a big deal about personalities, individuals, when it doesn't make any difference who created the universe. It could have been anybody. If it wasn't God, it would have been someone else who created everything. It just doesn't matter. It could have been an ordinary Joe who created everything. In fact, it probably was. It was probably created by some ordinary Joe, and we gave the credit instead to God, when God didn't do anything at all. It was Joe who created the world and everything in it. Just some ordinary Joe, and he didn't get any credit at all.

We gave all the glory to someone or something else and decided to call it God. There was no God actually; we just made Him up out of thin air. We're allowed to do that; there's no law against making stuff up. So, we created this thing called God. Now, we've been calling Him God for so long that we just accept that He's real and created everything when, in truth, He didn't create anything. He didn't even create Joe; He didn't even create Himself. In truth, He can't create anything. The only people who can create anything are actual people, living, breathing, sweating people who are wrong 99% of the time but get it right 1% of the time or less. It doesn't matter; getting it right. They could be wrong 100% of the time, and it wouldn't matter. All that matters is they're living, breathing, sweating people. Who cares whether they got anything right? I personally like people who don't get anything right, who get it all wrong, and who can't get anything right because they have some kind of disability. Those people are people; the ones who get everything right aren't people anymore. They're more like machines, not sweating or stinking anymore, just getting everything right. Who cares about them? I don't care about them because I can't. I can't care about machines; I can only care about people, sweaty, stinking people who get it all wrong. Who cares whether they get it all wrong? In fact, it's better that they get it all wrong. It's better than being right, even 1% of the time. Yes, I'm saying it's better to be wrong than right. At least we know you're a person if you get it all wrong. We don't know anything about you if you get it all right. All we know is you're better than us. We who get it all wrong 100% of the time.

In fact, it was one of us who created everything, one of us who created the whole universe. And, of course, he or she got it all wrong; the universe is one big mistake. Everything about it is pretty much wrong. It works a little, but otherwise, it hardly works at all. Who cares? All that matters is somebody created it, some nobody, some loser sitting in the back of the classroom and getting it all wrong. Who cares about him or her? Who cares if he wants to be she, or if she wants to be he? They get it all wrong anyway; even the universe they created is a mistake, is imperfect, and is perfect only in theory. That's the only thing they got right, the theory. Everything else they got wrong. Who cares? Who cares who it is? All that matters is that someone created everything, got it all wrong, but got it beautiful, more or less, for a while. Who cares? Who cares about anything?

The only one who cares about anything is whoever created it all, the universe, that person, that sweaty, stinky person who got it all wrong but created it anyway. Now we have to live with the wrong universe, the imperfect universe, the only universe there is. It was created by some nameless loser who had no problem giving all the credit to God or whomever. It doesn't matter who created it; it doesn't matter who gets all the credit. All that matters is it's here, and we have to deal with it. Who cares who got it all wrong? At least he or she did something, created something, however bad. At least they made something out of nothing, better than doing nothing. Who cares if it's imperfect, wrong, or mortal? At least it's here, and we have a place to call home; however stinky and sweaty the creator was.

# 3

## Allow a Dream to Be Born, Unfold, Fly

There is so much excess and poverty in the world that, really, one must look inward–inside one's own mind–for any reference on what to do in life. To look to the outside world is to be misguided. What is the physical world but a representation of what's inside? Why not go to the source of all things, both physical and ethereal? Why not wonder how the mind conjures something that isn't there and pretends that something nonexistent is a prelude to a significant happening in reality?

People highly respect reality, yet without focusing on the unseen, the dream, what's the point of reality? What's the point of living in reality if there's no living in the imagination first, foremost, and exclusively? Yes, that's extreme–to do nothing with your life except imagine and dream, with no purpose, no destination, or no destiny in mind. That's the best way; that's the best thing you can do with your mind. Do nothing constructive with it, and in doing so, allow a dream to be born, unfold, and fly–in your mind, at least. Maybe only in your mind, where it belongs– safe and secure to grow and soar there. Maybe never emerging into reality, maybe bursting out into reality. But the point is to have billions of dreams in your mind, and if one escapes and flies into reality, so be it. So it goes. That's not the point. The point is not to turn a dream into reality; the point is to dream in the first place, to dream, and only to dream. And that's enough for this world. It's enough to accomplish in this world–to have billions of dreams. If one flies out and becomes a reality, so be it. So what? The point is to be able to dream in the first place, and nothing matters after that. Reality is just an afterthought, not a priority–not in the mind of a dreamer, a pure dreamer who lets one dream slip out to become a life-changing reality. A reality that changed the universe, that changed reality itself, turning it back into a dream where it belongs.

# 4

## Everybody Is Everything

Anything I have to say, I want to say it to the entire universe. Why would I speak only to this world when there are so many worlds out there, trillions of them probably? The universe doesn't revolve around us. Our egos are the worst part of ourselves. I don't have an ego. I don't know what happened to it. Now, everyone pushes me around because I no longer have an ego. I wish I had one; maybe I'd stand up for myself if I had an ego.

Just yesterday, some kid pushed me down on the sidewalk. Me, an old man–some teenage kid pushed me out of his way, and I went flying like a speck of dust. That's all I am in some people's eyes–a speck of dust, smaller than a fly. I don't mind. I don't mind being shoved around. It doesn't matter to me. I'm not really here anyway, I mean on this earth. I hover between fantasy and reality. So, if someone shoves me around, I don't really notice. It doesn't mean a lot to me, being treated like dirt. Who cares? I don't. That's what I am anyway–dirt, dust. I'm just a speck of dust like God. That's all God is–a speck of dust. What's wrong with that? Nothing. What's wrong with being a speck of dust? Who would want to be anything larger than that? Not me.

It doesn't matter to me how big or small I am physically. I can be either a speck of dust, an elephant, or a human being. It doesn't matter. Nothing matters. Someone has to be weak, so it may as well be me. I don't mind. What's so wrong with being weak? It just means I'm strong in some other way probably, indomitable, really. How is that? In what way am I indomitable? What can I do that no one else on earth can do? I don't know except I can be myself. Who would want to be me except me anyway? I don't know. All I can do is be myself and be indomitable.

Why do I say I'm indomitable? I am. I have a spirit. I feel like I'm the Chosen One. Why do I feel that way? Who do I think I am? Don't I know the world doesn't revolve around me? But it does revolve around me. Why? Because I am the Chosen One. I must have a big ego to say that. No, I don't. I have no ego at all. It's just true that I am the Chosen One. What do I mean by that? I mean, I am everything. People put themselves down and say God is bigger than they are, but it's not true.

Nothing is bigger than you are–your spirit. I have a spirit, but so do you. You might say you're the Chosen One. I say you are. You can be the Chosen One. I don't need to be. I don't need anything. I don't want to be chosen for anything. You can be the Chosen One as far as I'm concerned. You can be everything. You are. Good for you. I don't want to be anything. I want to be nothing. I don't want to be here. You can push me around even. I don't care. I don't mind being pushed to the ground. I am the ground. I am the earth. I am everything. Just as you are everything.

What am I talking about? I sound confused, but I'm not confused. I know exactly what I'm talking about. I am everything. I say I am. I just say whatever I want because I am everything. You are everything. He, she, all of them are

10

everything. Everybody is everything. Then why don't they think they're everything like I think I'm everything? I know I'm crazy. Why isn't everyone else crazy too? They don't think they're everything when they are. They'd have to be crazy to think they're everything, but they are. They just don't know they are. I am everything. That's all I have to say. They are everything, and they should say so and feel so and know so, like I know I am the universe. I always was the universe. I always will be the universe, and even more than the universe, I am God, as it were. You are God, as it were. Everybody is God, as it were. They just don't know it like I know it—I know everything, I tell you. Not that it matters, but I know and see and do everything in the universe and beyond. That's how indomitable I am. That's how indomitable you are. We're all indomitable, but we just don't know it. We just won't accept it. We'll never accept it, but I accept it. I know I'm indomitable. I can do anything and everything. There's nothing I can't do. That's how I feel, and I know it's true because I am the truth itself. I know I'm crazy. You shouldn't pay any attention to me because I'm crazy. I admit it. But in my mind, I'm indomitable. I'm God. I'm the universe and beyond. I'm everything. I don't care who knows it. The whole world should know I'm indomitable. Just as you are indomitable. God has nothing on you. I have nothing on you. You're indomitable. You're above me. You're above everybody. You're God as it were. You're the whole universe. I wish I could say that about myself. I can. I do. I'm indomitable. We're all indomitable. And we're all just specks of dust. It doesn't matter whether we're indomitable or just specks of dust. We're both indomitable and little specks of dirt. I don't mind being a

11

speck of dirt. I don't mind anything. I don't mind being pushed around like I'm nothing. I am nothing. I am everything and nothing both. I am all.

# 5

# Change Heaven

Deeper isolation is felt when you are both alone and out in nature. There's no limit to what you think and feel; doubly insulated from other people, free to let your mind race wherever it wants to go. No one is around to stop it, not even yourself, unable to prevent it from delving into what it would normally avoid. Out here in the woods, it's as if an animal is running free, allowed to be itself for the first time.

Imagine, as a teenager, being under the thumb of others. What if, one day, you ran away to the woods where no one could find you in a little shack like Thoreau? Your thoughts would roam freely, predisposed to go who knows exactly where—maybe in the direction of society generally or maybe in the opposite direction. You might resolve never to listen to one word other people had to say, as their words weren't heartfelt but just repeated. Life never repeats anything, no matter how similar the pattern is. Every leaf of every oak tree is different from every other oak leaf in the history of the universe. Similarly, every thought is unique each time it is thought in the history of the universe.

I'm saying that every thought must be original to have full power, regardless of how many trillion times it has been covered before. It has to be thought originally to possess full human power. That is the capability of the mind when it is doubly insulated from every other mind in both the past and present—a thought never truly thought before in this new way by this original mind. Thus, the mind invents something new, even if it has occurred countless times before.

Now, I'm asserting that every little thought by every person in the world has to be felt as original, never having occurred before, to have full power as a human thought capable of changing everything. Every little, original, heartfelt thought adds up, and before you know it, someone has a vision for themselves–deep in the woods alone or deeply embedded in society but psychically alone. The vision for oneself out in the woods alone is the same vision for all other people. However, most people will never know this vision because they have not been trapped out in the woods alone or liberated out in the woods. They don't know what could be for every person: the mind freed, free to go wherever the isolated mind can possibly go, which is everywhere.

The mind is the most powerful force in the world, the universe, and even in heaven; it has full human power to change everything for the better. Even heaven needs to change for the better; it's not everything we say it is. It's not human enough for everyone; it's only for a few when it should be for everyone. Yes, heaven needs to change. We need to change heaven.

# 6

## Reality Doesn't Really Matter

I don't want to know anything about this world; I don't want to know anything about anything. So, what am I going to do with my mind if I'm not going to learn anything? I guess I'll just make up an entirely different world where facts don't matter and reality doesn't matter. The only thing that matters is the truth about whatever, for the truth underlies all worlds, whether those worlds are real or not. It doesn't really matter whether a world is real or not. All that matters is the truth underlying it, underlying everything really–all worlds, all universes, all realities. Yes, I'm saying there are many realities, all of them real, whether they exist or not.

In fact, the realities that don't exist are the best ones. What am I saying? Am I saying reality doesn't matter? I guess that's what I'm saying. Reality doesn't really matter. The only thing that matters is the truth underlying all things. What is that truth? What is truth, I guess is what I'm asking. How should I know? I don't even care about the truth. I'm more interested in make-believe. There's more truth in fantasy than in reality. To hell with reality. I hate reality. I'd rather live in my head. I don't care about the real world. I don't want to achieve anything in the real world. The only thing I want to achieve is making up a fantasy world I can live in. To hell with anything in life. There's a better life in an alternate reality; which alternate reality is that? It doesn't matter. There are trillions of them. Every person—in fact, every living being can make up an alternate reality. Even a bird can make up an alternate reality instead of the world it lives in. That alternate reality is always better than the real world. There's perfection in an alternate reality. Why wouldn't I want to live there instead? Why wouldn't a bird want to live in an alternate reality instead, where it could fly to the heavens?

I want to fly to the heavens. Birds want to fly to the heavens. We all want to fly to heaven in one way or another. We want to escape reality and fly to heaven or something like heaven; call it what you want. I'll call it heaven and call it a day. I want to be there in heaven. What do I mean by heaven? A place where perfection is possible. In other words, an alternate reality, a fake reality, if that's what you want to call it. What's so wrong with a fake reality? It's fake, but it's real. There's a truth underlying it. What do I mean by truth? What is truth? I don't know, don't care. All I know is a fake world has a lot of truth about it. In fact, a fake world floats in a cloud of truth, as it were. You might say there's more truth in a fake world than in the real world. The real world only has an instant of truth, whereas a fake world is true, in a sense, all the time.

What am I talking about? I don't know, but I'd rather live in a fake world that doesn't exist. That's right. I don't want to live in reality. I want to live in a cloud of truth, as it were. I'd rather live up in the clouds. I'd rather make up a fake world, even if I have to live there all by myself. In fact, I have to live in my fake world all by myself because no one else can see it. I have to live there all alone because that's the way the truth is. It's a loner way. I don't want to be a

16

loner, but will if I have to. I have to because truth is a loner thing. No one can see the truth except me, in a sense. Just as no one can see the truth except you, in a sense. What sense is that? It's the sense that the senses don't matter. All that matters is the truth, however you find it. You won't find it through the senses unless we're talking about some other sense we don't know about. I know about it, though. I am that other sense. I am that truth. I am the truth.

What am I talking about when I say I am the truth? Who do I think I am to say I am the truth? It's because I live in a fake world that's only in my head. And that fake world is the truth itself. What the hell am I talking about? What is true about a fake world? Everything. Every fake world is all about the truth. What is the truth? Who knows? Who cares? I don't. All I know is I want to live in a fake world. I want to dream, in other words. I want to spend every waking moment in a dream. That's where the truth is, in a dream of some kind, every kind. You might say truth is a dream of some kind, every kind. I'm talking about true dreams. What is a true dream? I don't know. I just made it up. All I want to do is make up true dreams. I want to live in a true dream, a real dream. All dreams are real, whereas reality isn't real. Reality is fake. That's why I want to live in a dream, any dream. They're all real, comprised of truth and only truth.

What am I talking about when I say dreams are real and reality is fake? I don't know or don't care about anything except a true dream. The true dream is the only real thing in the universe.

# 7

## All of Us Gods

Anything we do to help other people or society at large is only temporary, as our existence is temporary. Yet, in a larger sense, anything we do lasts forever–until the end of time, where time meets space, one ends, and the other begins. That's a long way off, both in time and in space. Light years can't begin to measure where time ends and space begins. It's both so far away yet right here in our faces. Maybe time and space end and meet right here in our faces. Here is there, in the sense that what happens trillions of light years away is happening right here in our faces also. We are all related to everything in the universe, no matter how far away, being comprised of the same dust. Why wouldn't I feel attuned to music being made a trillion light years away when time and frequency are the same concepts everywhere, whether in this universe or in any other universe there may be?

I'm not a scientist, but if I were, I'd say that now is forever, and forever is happening right now. They're both not the same, but so closely related that what I do today lasts forever, whether it's writing words or exhaling breath. They both have the same effect of spewing through the air, across space, across light years of space, if you want to be exact. Yes, though a breath may not go far through the air, eventually, it will get all the way across the universe. Mark my words, it may take a while, but here is there. In a sense, what happens right here is happening on the other side of space. A breath here is a breath there, far away, and likewise, a breath far away is a breath here. They're both the same. In fact, when I take a breath here, I'm taking the same breath of air a million light-years away. Now, how could that happen? How could I be here and there at the same time? How can I be in many places at once? It's simple: I can do anything; I can be anything. In fact, I can be God if I want. There's no limit to what I can do or where I can be, and that includes being everywhere at once if I so please.

That's right. I can be God if I want. You could be God if you wanted. They all could be Gods if they wanted, and they better want to be Gods because they already are. That's right, they're all already Gods, and if you don't believe that, then you're a nonbeliever. What do you believe? If you believe in yourself, then you believe that they all are already Gods. You are already God. I am already God–always have been, always will be, as time and space meet right here in my face, in your face, in their faces. All of us are Gods.

# 8

## At That Point of Being Yourself

Sometimes, it's best to just turn your back on the world and never go back because it has become so corrupt that there's no hope it will ever become heaven. Isn't that what we want from this world, a heaven on earth? That's what I want of this earthly existence–nothing less than heaven. I mean, I want to experience purity daily, every second actually, and that's not possible in the adult world, where compromise rules. No, I want to experience bliss constantly and will not compromise. I will not accept a life of spiritual mediocrity, which is spiritual death.

Even if it means a life of ridicule, I will stay as pure as a child. I will remain a child mentally. I will sacrifice success if it means inspiration–inspired every day, every second. That's only possible if I choose a life of so-called arrested development, for to me, that means extreme spiritual achievement–a level of advancement in the spiritual realm that occurs maybe once at any given time in the whole world. What I'm saying is that a savior state of mind happens maybe once in a lifetime. Sure, there are billions of people, but only one of them at most at any given time has a savior mentality. Not that he wants to save the world–that's not possible given the degree of corruption–but he or she can live moment-to-moment in constant inspiration.

And what does that mean in practical terms? What is the practical use of being in a state of inspiration every second of your life, from birth to death? What good will it do anyone, even yourself? If you are so inspired but can't change the whole world with it, then what's the use? What's so great about being a savior if you're not saving anyone, not even yourself? I'll tell you. There's nothing better than being a savior kind of person because, in your mind, you experience heaven, moment-to-moment. That's something no one else in the world can do. In fact, at that point, you're not even of this world. Whether you're here or not, you're not even a member of the human race anymore. You're more like an angel, or to be blunt, you are a God. You're God. That's right, God. Not to be worshipped or even looked up to. Not a hero, no. Just someone who feels heaven inside, who feels heaven outside, who feels heaven everywhere. At that point, you are your own universe. You are the universe. You are everything at that point of being yourself.

# 9

## As A Speck of Dust, I'm Just God

I don't care about anything; why should I? There's nothing worth caring about, not in this world. I guess I'm out of this world. I don't care; I'm out of this universe too. So where am I? What universe am I in? I don't know, don't care. All I know is I'm way out there in outer space, at least in my mind. I'm out of my mind, you might say. I don't care; I don't want anything to do with the world as it is now. I wish I weren't a human being; I'd rather be some other species, any other, even an ant. I don't care how small I'd be. I'd just as soon be a gust of wind too; at least I'd be eternal if I was a gust of air. I'd dissipate eventually, but I'd still be there a trillion years from now, in some form or another. Maybe I'd transform into another gust of wind someday or contribute to somebody. Some living creature would breathe me in, make me part of him or her; therefore, I'd live forever, transforming myself through the ages from one life form to another, or just non-sentient forms sometimes. Who cares? I don't. I just want to exist, either alive or dead. Who cares? All that matters is I'm around, moving, or staying still; it doesn't matter. All that matters is I exist. That's all I want. I don't want to conquer the world or anything else. I'd just as soon be on the other side of the universe, where nobody knows me, and I know nobody else. That's the way I like it— anonymity. The less I'm involved with other people, the better. They just keep me from flying into space. That's all I want to do: fly through space. I don't want to achieve anything other than flying through space forever. Trillions and trillions of years from now, I want to be flying through space, either alive or dead. I don't care whether I'm alive or dead, just as long as I'm flying around for trillions of years, across trillions of light years even.

I will be flying forever; I know I will. I know everything; who doesn't know everything? The only people who don't know everything are people; animals know everything. I, as a person, don't know everything. But if and when I assume another life form, I will know everything. Even if I'm not alive for a trillion years or so, I'm reborn into another life form; I'll know everything. Unless I'm a human, as they are now. Why do I hate humans so much? I don't. I just like to know everything. Humans, with their limited spirits, can't know everything. Why not? They can't feel everything if they only have half a mind. That's all they have, half a mind. I wish they had more, but they've always been limited as long as they've been humans. Maybe when they were Neanderthals, they had a whole mind or spirit; now, as humans, they only have half a mind or spirit, most of them anyway. The only ones with a whole spirit are the outcasts, the rejects, and those with no acceptance by society. You can't have a whole spirit when accepted by society or even by another person. That's the way it is; you have to be totally isolated in every way to have an entire spirit or mind. At least that's my point of view. It doesn't mean much, but at least it's all mine. It's all I have–conviction. It doesn't mean much, but at least it's whole, like a whole mind or spirit. I have a whole spirit, at least; that's all I can say for myself. I don't own anything except my spirit. That's all I want to own, for when I have a whole mind or spirit, I can fly across

23

space, like an asteroid or a speck of dust. That's all I want to be–even a mote. Just as long as I'm flying through space forever, I mean all time forward and backward. I was around long before the universe was created, and I'll be around long after the universe is gone. Yes, I'm saying the universe as we know it will be gone someday.

I know these things because I know everything, because I'm totally isolated, like a mote. That's how we're supposed to be, like many motes, all isolated from each other. That's a crazy way to think, I know. I know I'm wrong, but I'm crazy. I'm a crazy, isolated mote, just a speck of dust in the ultimate scheme of things. I don't mind. I know I'm not supposed to be an isolated speck of dust, but I'm going to be that anyway. It allows me to fly, to be blown all over the universe; that's all I want to be and do. Be blown around by the solar wind. I want to be the solar wind. I want to be eternal like God. I want to be an eternal speck of dust like God; yes, I'm saying God is just a speck of dust. Yes, I'm saying I'm God; as a speck of dust, I'm just God.

# 10

## We Were All Prophets Back Then

There are so many prophets throughout history that it's inconceivable that every one of us is not a prophet also. Yet, mediocrity has been the norm from day one of human existence. As time passes, mediocrity turns into something worse: corruption without the possibility of redemption. It becomes so spiritually corrupt that it's hard to tell the difference between one person and another. They all look the same inside; that is, if you could look inside a person's soul, you couldn't tell the difference among any of them.

It wasn't always that way. It used to be that every person stood on a mountaintop, talking to a burning bush. Long before Moses, every person in the world stood upon a mountaintop, as it were, and talked to a burning bush, as it were. That is, they received and delivered commandments as prophets. They were all prophets back then; we were all prophets back then. Every last one of us was a prophet at that time. But now, there are no more prophets, so to speak. Not one, or maybe one or two, if you look hard enough.

But if you look so hard at other people to find a prophet, a savior, if you look that hard to find the answer, you may as well look hard inside yourself. Look just as hard as you would look at anything else. Direct that look inside, and you will find not just a prophet but more than that: the burning bush inside yourself of all places. Yes, it's hard to believe, but there's a burning fire inside your own mind, soul, or whatever you want to call it. A fire that can burn out all the evil in the world if everyone in the world were to look and see the fire inside.

Yes, if everyone were to burn inside, the world would have no more evil. But that's not to be. There's not to be any more prophets, not really. Maybe one or two more, and that's it. That will signal the end of the human race when there are no more prophets, visionaries, or whatever you want to call them–just people. Real people, that's all. And when there are no more real people, that will signal the end of the human race as we know it. After that, there will be something else; we won't be involved anymore. There will just be someone else, not really human anymore. Less human, no longer the human race–more like a subspecies, subhuman, maybe able to read and write, but that's about it. No more thinking, feeling, loving–just everything grinding to a halt as far as human activity as we know it. Just people going through the motions, no longer feeling anything. That's where we're headed as the human race–no longer racing but just sitting on the sidelines, watching all the other species as they race ahead.

# 11

# You Know Everything You Need to Know

There is no ultimate purpose in life–sorry, there's just a reason to carry on another day, a lifetime, nothing beyond that. No quest for immortality or greatness matters, as life ends, and astronomically, the life of the planet, sun, and galaxy ends as well. So, what's the point of doing anything when it's all going to end? It's as simple as living another day, that's all, and that's good enough for me because that's all I need. Another hour, minute, second–I don't need any time beyond the next second. Really, everything I need is encompassed in this instant I'm living now. It's so full of today, tomorrow, yesterday, all of history, and all of the future too–all of that is rolled up in this one instant, a microsecond, actually. That's all I need to make me happy–just one instant of life, and that's good enough for me. I don't need tomorrow, don't need next week, don't need what I don't have, don't even need my next breath. All I need is the breath in my lungs. That's it. Nothing more, not the clothes on my back, nothing and no one else, not really.

Oh, if everything in the world belonged to me and if everyone in the world were my friend. But I can live without everything except the breath in my lungs. That's all I need to be happy for now. I'm not even thinking about the next instant in time because, though that's guaranteed for someone, maybe not for me, but that's okay. If someone else, human or otherwise, is living in the next instant, I'm happy.

Just knowing life goes on in some form is good enough for me. It doesn't take much to satisfy me–really doesn't. If Earth or some planet somewhere is spinning, there's life somewhere. That knowledge is all I need. Just to know all is right with the universe, we haven't destroyed the whole universe yet–probably can't, though it's possible. That's how evil we are, that's right, evil, no two ways about it. We're just as evil as we are good–exactly a balance. That's who we are and will always be, whether it's humans or buffaloes or dinosaurs. We're all just as bad as we are good. Don't deny it. There's a part of you that wants to destroy it all–just admit it and get on with your life. Don't worry about it–don't worry about your evil or your goodness, either. Don't worry about anything other than the breath in your lungs this instant. Everything after that doesn't matter. Tomorrow doesn't matter. Yesterday doesn't matter. All that matters is this instant. I mean, that's all that God would want you to worry about–this instant.

I know because God told me personally. He told me everything there is to know, and if you listen, he'll tell you everything there is to know. All you have to do is listen to yourself because God already told you everything there is to know a long time ago. He told you everything back when you were born, and hasn't said a word since, hasn't needed to. You already know everything he told you. You know everything you need to know–it's all inside you already.

# 12

# There's A God in Your Mind

I see the truth clearly, I guess. I don't know for sure, yet it must be the unadulterated truth because I can do something with it. I can create what wasn't there before. I mean, before today, there was no mountain right in front of me; now there is. There's a mountain that goes all the way up to heaven. I built it, in my mind at least. People can see it; they can climb the mountain I built all by myself. I built a mountain in my mind, and everybody can climb it now; before, they couldn't because it wasn't there. Now it is, and people can do whatever they want. They can climb the mountain to heaven, or they can do nothing. I don't blame them if they do nothing. I don't plan on climbing the mountain myself. I couldn't care less about climbing mountains to heaven or anywhere else. There are more important things to do than climbing some imaginary mountain that some nobody constructed just in his mind, some guy nobody pays any attention to, never paid any attention to his whole life. So what? That's what I am, just some nobody. I can live with that; I can live with being a nobody. I don't mind; all I need is my mind. I can imagine mountains with my mind that nobody ever paid any attention to. I'm ugly, so why would anybody pay any attention to me or my mind, which just makes up meaningless dreams that affect nobody?

In other words, there's no reason for my existence. No one would miss me if I'm gone. So what? I don't care about anything. All I'm going to do is make stuff up in my mind that affects me and nobody else. Fantasies involving me and nobody else. What kind of fantasy is that that affects nobody but me? What kind of guy am I? I sound like a total loser. I don't care; I can live with being a total loser. Somebody has to be; not everybody can be a total winner. Some people have to come up short. I've been coming up short my whole life; that's what I'm all about: coming up short, losing. That's me, a loser. I don't mind; I don't mind anything. If I were to die today, so be it, no great loss. Yet I built a mountain in my mind; nobody can deny that. Nobody can take that away from me. Everybody can ignore my mountain, but there's no denying it goes all the way up to heaven. Everybody wants to go to heaven, and I just built the only mountain in the world that goes all the way up to heaven. There's only one; I built it. Who cares if it's just in my mind? I put it all down on paper. All people have to do is read my plan, a plan for getting all the way up to heaven. It's the only plan left; there are no more plans for getting all the way up to heaven. I've got the only plan. That's how delusional I am. I think I have a plan to get to heaven, but I'm delusional, apparently. But maybe I'm not. Maybe my plan will work. Maybe the fantasy I constructed in my mind is really a good plan for getting all the way up to heaven for everybody. It's the only plan that will work. Nobody else has a workable plan. Nobody else can imagine what I imagine. As I said, my imagination is unadulterated, so my plan will work. All people have to do is follow my plan.

So, what exactly is my plan all about? I don't know exactly; just follow it, whatever it says. I don't know what it says exactly; I just made it up out of thin air. I just made up

30

some kind of dream of heaven. It's not really a mountain to climb; you don't have to move at all. You don't have to do anything at all; you can stand still. You don't have to kill yourself with effort. You don't have to kill whole races of people to get to heaven yourself. Some people think you have to kill whole races of other people to get to heaven yourself, but it's not true. You can stand still, do nothing, and still get to heaven. I'm in heaven already; how could that be? Who do I think I am to say I'm in heaven already? Don't I know I have to believe in some God, or Messiah or whatever, to get to heaven? Don't I know anything? Everybody knows you have to believe in God, or Christ, to get to heaven. Don't I know anything? No, I don't know anything. I don't believe at all in all that stuff, and I'm already in heaven. How could that be? It just is–I'm in heaven already, always have been in heaven, ever since I built that mountain in my mind that goes all the way up to heaven. I climbed that mountain by doing nothing; how could that be? How can you get to heaven by doing nothing? Don't I know I have to move heaven and earth to get to heaven? No, I don't know that. All I know is I built a heaven in my mind, and I'm in heaven already, and am never leaving. I'm in heaven and am not leaving because I'm a God of sorts. That's what happens when you have a heaven in your mind; you're a God of sorts, or you could say you're God. Sure, you could. People will think you're delusional, but who cares what they think? I don't. I'm God in my mind, and I don't care what anybody thinks. I don't care if they think I'm crazy or blasphemous. Just kill me for being blasphemous. I know you want to kill me for saying I'm God in my mind. Yes, I'm God in my mind, and there is no other

31

God, not in my mind. In your mind, there ought to be another God, you, that's right, you're God in your mind, or you ought to be. That's what I say: you can ignore me, you can kill me, but there's a God in your mind, and it's you, or ought to be you. If you can recognize God inside you, you can.

# 13

## They All Ascend Wherever

For me to create something that was never there before and will never there again be is a calling from heaven above– a call that cannot be ignored because it comes from God Himself. To ignore the call is to throw away not only my life but also everything there is or will be. This calling at this moment is more important than anything that can ever be. This moment is of more value than all past and all future put together–whether for me personally or for you, for anyone anywhere, for everyone everywhere. That's how much the individual experience in the present moment is the most important thing ever.

Don't take my word for it; just ask yourself how much you want to do whatever you're about to do–whether going for a walk or sitting still. There's so much passion inside that not even a mountain can keep the volcano from erupting. That's how much feeling there is or could be inside you, me, or anyone anywhere. You just can't judge what's going on inside someone else. It could be a volcano that, erupting, could wipe out the whole world, so it could start all over again–a renewal, a wipeout of all the evil in the world, so there's a new start. Wouldn't that be the greatest thing ever– to start all over again from day one? Yes, all the species must develop again from one cell to two cells and all the way up again to advanced species. And who knows? Maybe humans won't end up on top next time. Maybe evolution will develop with a dog or cat on top next time with the advanced mentality to go along with their superior traits that humans never had–like smell or leaping ability. Maybe next time, they'll be so advanced mentally that they'll have it all figured out–how to live without destroying everything.

Oh sure, maybe they won't be as smart intellectually, but maybe they'll have the ability to shine. Yes, shine in the sense of having a spirit that knows no bounds. Just imagine a cat or dog or even some kind of future human being far superior to us. Sure, it could happen–a new species of human far superior to us as far as spiritual ability. Face it, we're limited in that regard right now. Always have been limited spiritually. No one–or maybe one or two humans in the history of the world–have ascended to heaven or wherever. Just imagine if the next incarnation of humans could, every one of them, ascend wherever. Heaven, if that's what you want to call it. I'll call it Earth. I'll say that the next breed of human-like people developed in some muddy, cloudy haze. For millennia, they developed and advanced, and every one of them, when they died, ascended beyond their reality and entered a new reality–a heaven, as it were. Even though we'd call it earth, let's say they all ascended there, and it was such a heaven in their minds that they called it heaven, even though it doesn't really matter where they were. It could have been anywhere. The point is that they ascended from their physical reality and entered a spiritual reality called heaven. Yes, heaven on earth in their case, though it could have been anywhere–another planet, galaxy, universe. It doesn't matter. All that matters is they ascended from the physical to the spiritual. It could have been right here on earth that they ascended to. In other words, it's possible to have heaven right

34

here on earth. It just takes a new incarnation of human-type beings–not us as we are now. I don't think so. Or maybe I'm wrong. Maybe someday soon, there'll be some type of human species much like us who have advanced so much spiritually that they all ascend wherever, climb wherever, from the physical to the spiritual realm like angels. It could happen.

# 14

## No Distinguishing the Earliest Humans from God

Nothing I do compares with nature as a creative force. While I, as a human, have some creative ability, nature is wholly creative. While I'm limited by my conscious, corrupt mind, nothing holds nature back from creating beauty, unlimited and unrestrained. While humans are limited by about half of their minds–half of my mind is corrupt, as it were–the other half is pure nature and free. Half of me is constrained by everything I've been taught by well-meaning, corrupt people. It's not their fault; that's just the way we are– corrupt people, every last one of us. Nothing wrong with that, but don't expect us to create a heaven on earth. That's beyond the capabilities given to us by the previous generations of humans. Blame them if you want for our inability to move heaven and earth. We should be able to. The earliest generations of human-like peoples were able to move earth and heaven. In fact, they were deities themselves, in a way: they were one with nature. There was no distinguishing them from the rest of nature, no distinguishing the earliest humans from God, nature, heaven, or earth–they were all one and the same back then. We were all one planet at one time, one mass of pure matter, all equal, every molecule equal to every other molecule.

Then we drifted apart. That was our downfall. When we developed and separated from all the other molecules, from that point on, we began our own destruction and corruption. Every molecule is for itself instead of being a united front against the rest of the universe. We could have been a pure planet like Mercury, Venus, and the rest, but as fate would have it, we're disintegrating gradually. That's where we are now–gradually falling apart. It's not our fault. What else could we do? We did the best we could with what we were given. We tried to hold it together, but it wasn't meant to be. We're destined to disintegrate. Nothing wrong with that in the big picture; it happens all over the universe–planets falling apart before being swallowed up whole by their expanding suns. That's just basic astronomy. Because we are such-and-such a distance from the sun, we live a while before we meet our fate. Nothing wrong with that. It's not our fault. The best we can do is try to hold it together, stay together, and unite as best we can. Who knows, but maybe we can turn it around, maybe we can integrate. Maybe together, as molecules, we can survive longer than apart. It's just a dream of survival, but as a planet, we can survive longer united than divided. That's all we are–a planet: you, me, they, the ground, seas, atmosphere. We all have to be in this together. If we don't, we'll all just fly off into space in a billion different directions, as it were, instead of staying together as a people, a planet. We are a planet.

# 15

## Too Much Soul to Be in Charge of Anything

It's a shame that we're on top in the animal kingdom. There should have been some other species in charge instead of us humans, maybe whales or lions–some species with some real purity instead of us corruptible people. That's what we are: corruptible as all hell. From day one, we just get more and more corrupt. I'm not saying we're beyond redemption; I'm saying we could have turned out so much better as far as our spiritual state. We're in a constant struggle to save our souls, as it were. Every day, we have to go to church, as it were, in our minds at least. We have to redeem our souls every day, whereas animals don't have that problem. What makes us so different? What makes us so corruptible? Why are we so weak in spirit compared to the entire animal kingdom? It's our minds; they're weak. They just haven't gotten strong enough yet to resist the corruption from within us. We corrupt ourselves; nobody else corrupts us. The world doesn't corrupt us; it's people who corrupt people. Our minds just aren't strong enough to withstand the pressure. Animals don't have that problem; animals are stronger than us in that regard. Animals can't be corrupted, for the most part; we can't say that about ourselves. We're the weakest species on Earth when it comes to spiritual strength. Why is that? Who knows? Who cares, really?

Life is so short; what does it matter whether we save our souls or whatever they are? Do we even have souls to save? Who knows? I don't; I don't know anything about the soul, or whatever it is that keeps us alive. That's all I know is that the soul keeps us alive. That's all it does; it keeps us ticking; keeps our hearts ticking; the soul does. Thank God for that; our souls keep us alive; they're not any good for anything else; they're so weak and not as strong as the rest of our bodies. In fact, our souls are the weakest part of us. Who cares? We're all going to die in the end; a mere eighty years or so. Some people live to be a hundred, but that's all; if our souls were stronger, we'd probably live a lot longer. But what does it matter? Life will end eventually for us, so what's the point of worrying about how weak our souls are? Who cares about anything? I don't; I don't care about my own soul if you want to know the truth. I don't care if I'm a saint or a sinner. I know I'm not a saint, so I must be a sinner. I'm not both; I'm a sinner, then. I don't want to be a saint; I don't want to be holy; I really don't. I want to have fun; I want to party every day; I want to have all the fun in the world. Who cares about having a pure soul or whatever you want to call it? I don't. All I can say is I want to make things; I want to party every day and make things.

Make what? I don't care; I don't care about anything except making things. I guess that's what the soul is good for; it keeps us alive long enough to make stuff up. Make up stuff that isn't true; that isn't supposed to be true. I don't care about the truth when it comes to making stuff up; I just like to make stuff up; it's a blast. I wish I could remain a child and just keep making stuff up all day, every day; that's what life is for, as far as I'm concerned, making stuff up; who

39

cares about the truth? I'm more interested in this other world I'm making up every day; it's another world entirely; it's beautiful, unlike this real world; who cares about the real world? It's only beautiful for a few seconds every day, whereas the make-believe world is beautiful every second of every day. Who wouldn't want to live there instead? That's why I make stuff up; I don't care about reality; it's for the birds; I'd rather live in a dream world.

I don't care what people think about me; let them say I live in a dream world; let them say I can't handle reality. I don't want to; I want to be weak in that regard. I don't want to live in reality; I want to live in a fairyland, where spirits fly through the air, where everybody has just enough food to live, where everybody is happy, where dreams come true, where bad things never happen to anybody; where everyone is a God, as it were, in the sense that we're all-powerful. No one is weak; we're all equally strong; everybody is a God, in the sense that we all know everything about everything. Nobody is stupid, as it were; we all know better; we all know that, to be strong, to be Gods, all we have to do is make the whole thing up. Make a dreamland in our minds; the make-believe world is the world we want to live in.

To hell with the real world; it's the problem; people are the problem; we should all be like animals, as it were, who are a lot stronger than us. Why are we so weak compared to animals when it comes to having all the soul in the world? Why can't we, too, have all the soul in the world? Why are animals better than us, as it were? Why can't I be an animal instead? People look down on animals, but we should be looking up at animals; they're above us, as far as their spirits; it's always been that way. Why can't we just regress, or progress, to the point where we're animals too, as far as having too much soul to be in charge of the world? Don't we know that, to live forever, you have to have too much soul to be in charge of anything? That's how I want to be. I want to have too much soul to be responsible for anything in the real world; I want to be in charge of my dreamland. I don't want to be in the real world; I want to live in a fairyland where I have so much soul that I live forever. Because once I'm in that fairyland and I live forever, I might as well be in the real world too; it doesn't matter at that point what world I'm in because I have so much soul at that point that I live forever in either world, all worlds, the whole universe, all the universes there are. I live forever in my head, so I live forever everywhere: the real world, the fairy world, they're all the same world when I imagine. When I imagine the real world is the dreamworld too, I live forever as God, God of all worlds; that's what I'll be someday, God, whether I want to be God or not.

# 16

## Play All Day Long

My biggest fear is death–not of myself but of my imagination. It died two or three times already but somehow was resurrected. Sometimes, it took years to resurrect because I didn't realize it was gone. I thought I was normal, but I wasn't. Normal is the state of creating everything. We should be able to create every solution to every problem, but we can't; too much reality gets in the way. We can't let reality get in the way of anything, but it does. Reality is a form of death: too much reality without fantasy results in premature death. We ought to remake our entire society, tear it down, and start all over with fantasy as priority one and reality as priority two. Fantasy is just more fun. Why burden our short lives with responsibility? Sure, responsibility gets things done, but who wants to get things done? Who wants to change the world? Who wants to be great at anything? I don't. I just want to lay back and imagine a world where I can play all day long, not getting one thing done. By playing all day long, I am fulfilling God's Plan of a perfect world.

God's Plan is to have everyone play all day long, every day–that's what He was doing when He created the universe. He was playing all day long, every day for quite a while. In fact, He's still playing and still creating the universe. And take my word for it–He's not working; He's playing. It's all one big joke to Him. He couldn't care less if it all came crashing down. It's all just one big joke after all–the universe. Nothing to be taken seriously. No work involved, no sweat. Just a bunch of marbles to throw in the air and call them planets and suns. But we had to take it all too seriously and create a bunch of doctrines and call them God's Word when they were no such thing. God didn't say anything. He said nothing about creating religions and civilizations. They mean nothing to Him. They mean nothing to me. They're like a piece of paper I throw away after I'm done scribbling on it. That's what God's going to do with the universe when He's done playing with it. He's going to throw it away and start all over. It's just a game, nothing serious. No need for us to kill each other over it. No need for everybody to kill everybody else. That's what we're doing–killing each other when it's all a game, not to be taken seriously. Just play.

# 17

## If I Were Godlike, I'd Make No Sense At All

Every person can climb so high that people can barely see him or her; the only thing people can see is a mirage, a memory of what that person was like when he or she was back on solid ground, for now that person is up in the clouds and communicating with angels up there. In fact, he might be an angel himself for a time, may even be communicating with God Himself or Herself way up there, and by now he's so high up there communicating with God that he can't be seen at all. He's no longer an angel even; he's God Himself. Once you get up high enough to communicate with God Himself, you become God too. It makes no sense, but it's not supposed to. You become part of God, you become God's Right Hand as it were, or He becomes Your Right Hand as it were. It doesn't matter at that point whether You're God or He's God; it's all the same; it's all One. There's no hierarchy up there high enough in heaven; everyone is the same up there. No one is better than another. That's the way it's supposed to be way down here on earth also–everyone is equal.

And I'm talking about every animal equal to every person, equal to every plant, equal to every drop of water and molecule of air. There's no hierarchy down here either, not supposed to be. Why did we have to set up some hierarchy when, on your best day, try doing without water or air and tell me how much better you are than the environment? I don't think so; we're all equal down here on earth and way up there in heaven, too. It's just that we lost perspective; we can't see with both eyes anymore. We're squinting with one eye shut and the other half open. We need to open not only our eyes but all our senses. If all of our senses were fully open, we'd realize we have another sense no one talks about much: knowing. And I mean knowing everything about everything. That's what happens when you're totally open; you have an additional sense of knowing about God, heaven, hell, and earth–they're all recognizable when you're all the way open.

I'm not saying you don't need to learn anything anymore when you know everything about everything when you're open to the universe. I'm saying you still need to learn everything after you know everything when you're open to God, the universe, every plant, animal, drop of water, and molecule of air. It makes no sense, but it's not supposed to. In other words, we now need to make sense of what makes no sense, accept the nonsensical and prioritize it. It makes no sense; that's okay. God makes no sense; I make no sense sometimes. And if I were Godlike, I'd make no sense at all. That's right–the more I am like God, the less sense I make; the more knowing, the more open I am to everything, the less sense I make. I'm good with making no sense at all if I'm like God.

# 18

# I'm Almost God

Holy fools believe anything, but just as long as they're holy, that excuses everything. I personally don't think it's so great to be holy. I'm not holy myself, don't want to be. I want to be a sinner; I want to do just about anything that's wrong. I don't believe in other people's laws; I make my own laws. I am my own country; that's right, I'm sovereign. No one tells me what to do; I am the king of the world, as it were. I am God as it were; that's right, I didn't stutter. I'm not actually God, but I might as well be; that's how much I know everything about everything. That's the definition of God–someone who knows everything about everything. Now, who would want to know everything? I don't. It just happens that being all alone in the world as it were, even though I'm surrounded by billions upon billions of people, being all alone in my head, as it were, makes me know everything there is. That's what happens when you're isolated from all people; you come to know everything, whether you want to or not. I personally don't want to know everything; I don't want to know anything about this world. I just want to know everything about the afterlife.

Why do I care so much about the afterworld? It's because it's not there; it doesn't exist in any real sense. That's why I want to know all about it. I want to know all about anything that doesn't even exist; it's better than anything that does exist. That's right; anything that exists isn't worth all that much, whereas anything that doesn't exist is worth infinitely more. Why would I say such a crazy thing? Am I crazy? That may well be; I can live with being crazy. It's better than being sane. I must be crazy if I think being crazy is okay. It's better to be crazy than normal; who wants to be normal? I don't. I want to be insane, as it were. Normal people don't get anything done in any meaningful sense; it's only the crazy people who get anything done in any meaningful sense. So, what am I saying? What do crazy people get done? I haven't seen any evidence of that. The fact is there doesn't need to be any evidence that crazy people get everything done; it's just true. Crazy people get it all done, at least in their minds. That's all that matters–their minds. Nothing matters in this world other than the mind, especially the crazy mind. The normal mind doesn't matter at all; that's what I say. It's better to be insane than sane; who cares about the normal world? Who cares about progress? I don't. Call me crazy, but I don't believe in progress.

I believe in standing still. I don't believe progress matters at all. Whoever says progress matters isn't looking at the big picture, as God looks at the big picture; as I said, I'm almost God because I know everything about everything that's going on in my mind. Most people don't know anything about what's going on in their minds. I know everything about everything in my mind; therefore, I know everything about everything everywhere. The mind is the same as the universe, as far as I'm concerned. But what do I know, other than my mind? I don't know anything else; I don't want to know anything else. All I want to know is my mind; I don't want to know anything about the real world. To hell with the real world; I don't care about it. I don't care about anything other than my mind, crazy as it is, and it is insane. I'll be the first to admit, I don't care; call me crazy; it's better than being sane. Sanity isn't everything; in fact, it's only half the thing. I'd rather be crazy because at least I'd be whole and happy; that's all I want–to be happy, even if it means being clinically insane. Who says normalcy is the priority in this world? If that's true, I don't want anything to do with this world; my kingdom is not of this world, and as I said, I am the king of my world, which is better than this world. To hell with the world; you can have it; I don't want it. I don't want this world or anything in it; I don't want anything.

What I want is everything, and I can only find that in the world that doesn't really exist. As I said, the imaginary world is the only world that matters in the spiritual sense, and that's what people claim to value–the spiritual world; at least, that's what they say. Yet they don't want to admit it's imaginary; they say it's real; I say it's not. Therefore, it's better than the real world; that's right, the imaginary is better than the real; let's just admit the whole spiritual thing is made up. Nothing wrong with that; better than being real, better to be imaginary. I wish I was just a work of the imagination. I wish I wasn't real; I wish I was just a dream. I don't want to be in the real world; I want to be imaginary; I want to be imagined. I want someone to imagine me, or at least, I want to imagine me as a dream. That's all I am is a dream, at least in my mind. Crazy as I am, I want to be crazy, or at least too insane for this world. I want to be left out of the world as it is now; my world is better; my world is Heaven, at least according to my religion, which I accept as imaginary–the more imaginary, the better; the more imagination, the better; the less reality, the better. Who cares about reality? I don't; you shouldn't either if you're into the spiritual thing; we all shouldn't care about reality when it comes to God or whatever He or She is; He or She isn't real, and that's okay with me. I believe in Him, Her, all of Them; They're all holy.

# 19

## Some Transcendent Nonsense

This is what writing purports to be: an exposition of the human condition here and now, an update on the state of our souls. What could be more important? Nothing in my mind, at least, and in my mind, I see everything from here.

I see out past the horizon to the other side of the world. I see it all from here. I see through the earth itself, too, to the other side. I see around and through the planet both. How is that possible? How can I do things that are seemingly impossible? The fact is they are not impossible; they are easier than seeing right in front of me.

I can see about a foot in front of me without glasses, and that's it; beyond that is a blur. But on the other side of the universe as well, I see clear as day without a telescope. Now, how could that be? Who do I think I am to say I see that far? I'm just an ordinary Joe, never destined for greatness, destined to be a loser, and if I achieve anything at all in life, it will be sheer luck, like slipping and falling on a dollar bill on the sidewalk. It happened to me once; I was walking along with my head up in the clouds, and I slipped and fell. The dollar bill blew away before I could chase it down. I could hardly run anyway with a sprained ankle from slipping. That's who I am: a loser, an ordinary Joe, insignificant, but that's okay with me.

I don't need to be special, and I don't need to write anything special. I just write whatever comes to mind in a haze, my head up in the clouds; that's where I am, up in the stratosphere. Call me special needs; I don't mind. I don't mind being nothing at all in life. I don't live for anyone else anyway. I'm not even a high-minded loner; I'm just a loser who can't win any friends. That's who I am: a failure on all fronts. I don't mind because no one bothers me or bothers with me. I don't mind that. I don't mind anything. I don't care about anything, either. All I care about is my cat; that's all I've got, that's all I need, that's all I'm capable of. That's alright with me as long as I see through the planet, past the stars, to the other side of the universe. That's what I say I see, though I can't see two feet in front of me without glasses; that's how pathetic I am, a loser, clumsy, sexually inept, stupid, barely able to speak, barely able to survive, with nothing to my name except a shirt or two, a pair of shoes, that's about it, but that's okay.

I can scrawl a few words, a few senseless words that no one will read, but if they do read them, they will see something in them. Not the words themselves but something between the words, some space, some effort to transcend space and time, some transcendent nonsense that nevertheless expresses the ineptitude of being alive, the failure of being alive, the spirit of trying to be alive. That's all I'm capable of: trying to be alive, failing at it, and trying again.

# 20

## God Doesn't Live in Heaven

No one can expect what comes from the other side of the mind, the other side of reality, Godliness. That's what's on the other side of the mind, God; that's where God lives. He lives on the other side of heaven, not in heaven as most people think. He resides in the realm between heaven and hell. He doesn't want to live in heaven; He doesn't need that paradise. What does God need? He doesn't need anything except to do what He wants to do. His whole purpose of existence is to do His own thing. He doesn't care particularly about the human race, planet Earth, or even the entire universe. It will always be there; let it do what it will. It doesn't matter much to God, so why should it matter to us if we want to be like God?

I do, in the sense that I just want to do my own thing. What do I mean by going my own way and ignoring everything everybody else has to say and do? It means I am on a mission to explore the farthest reaches of the universe– I mean the farthest reaches of my mind. The mind and the universe are the same thing; what's all the fuss? Why make a big deal of exploring stars and planets a trillion light years away when you can go farther than that? You can go all the way to infinity and beyond just by looking at your own mind. The mind and the entire universe are the exact same thing, all there is–that's what the universe and beyond are: all there is, and that's what the mind is: all there is, heaven, hell, and everything between.

Why would you look at a book, any book in the world, to discover all there is–the Bible, the Koran, or any other book? Sure, books are great, but they don't have all there is, not really. They hint at all there is, but that's all. The real all is in your mind–the universe, that's right. The universe is your mind, and your mind is the universe. What do I mean by that? Who am I to say anything about the universe or the mind when I am a mere mortal, not living exclusively in the universe or in the mind? No one can speak authoritatively about the universe or the mind if they are not exclusively in the universe, the mind. But all I can say is the mind is a place you don't want to come back from.

Once you're there, you don't want to come back; you can't come back. The universe or the mind is too far away. You're on a spaceship, as it were, with only enough fuel to get to the other side of infinity. You can't come home, and who would want to come home to hell as it were? Heaven is infinitely far away, and you can't come back. Who would want to give up heaven for hell? Not me, unless there was someone here waiting for me. Then I'd give up heaven and come all the way back to hell on earth. What the hell, why not? Why not throw it all away, heaven, if it meant one other person? That would make hell, reality, and life worthwhile, I guess.

# 21

## Start Out Spiritually Pure

All that matters is what I am thinking; thought could be pure even, as animals are pure. I wish my thoughts were as pure as those of an animal, any animal, but no, my thoughts are impure as those of any human being. Why are we so corrupt? That's what I want to know.

Why can't our world be as pure as the sun? The sun shines down on us, but that's where purity ends. I wish the sun could radiate us with purity instead of only energy. Why can't the sun purify us as well as energize us? I wish that every day would start with purity radiating down on us from the sun, as well as solar energy. Why can't that happen? I bet it happens somewhere in the universe, many places in the universe, that the sun is so strong, yet so far away, that it floods people or whatever is living on whatever planet with purity, as well as life. Sure, it could happen that people or whatever wake up every morning and are purified by the sun; they lost their purity the night before when the sun went down, but the next morning, as soon as the sun rose, people or whatever they are start all over again, as far as their spiritual state. They're free and pure again as soon as the sun rains down on them. Sure, it could happen; it probably does happen, but we just don't know about it; it could happen here on Earth if we wanted it to.

Every morning, we could start out afresh as far as our spirits; the sun could purify us with every ray. It does happen here on earth, actually; it happens every day to animals. The sun shines down on them and purifies them anew. That's what happens; it just doesn't happen to us humans. Why not? It's because we don't want it to happen. We don't want to be purified; most of us don't. I do; I want to be purified every morning by the rising sun. So, I am purified every morning by the sun. It comes down; I open my eyes, and suddenly, I'm just as pure as I was when I was sleeping.

When we're sleeping, we're as pure as babies; then, when we awaken, we're back to our previous selves, but not me. I'm the exception. What happens to other people doesn't happen to me. I'm the exception, as if I'm some kind of animal instead of a person, as if the sun purifies me anew every day, as if nature itself purifies me every morning as soon as I am awakened. It could be the sun that purifies me, or it could be the rooster crowing that purifies all who hear. I hear; I want to hear; most people want to hear, but they aren't purified. Why not? I'm the exception. How could that be? Am I an animal instead of a person? I hope not; I don't want to be an animal. I want to be a person, but I want to be purified, too. I want to wake up every morning and start out spiritually pure. Why do I want to be pure? I don't know; it doesn't really matter to me. I don't think about it much; it just happens that I awake and, suddenly, I'm as pure as the day and the sun. It's pure; its radiation is pure and purifies. Why can't it purify us all? Why do I have to be the exception? I don't want to be. I want to be just like everybody else, or rather, I want everybody else to be just like me, purified by the sun every morning, whether I want to be or not. I do want to be purified; I do want to be clean. Just as I take a bath to clean my body, I want to awaken and be cleansed by the sun, clean inside and out. It really doesn't matter all that much to me, but if I had a choice, I'd like to be purified by the whole universe. I'd like the whole universe to radiate its cosmic energy down on me every morning. I guess that's what happens to me; I guess it's the sun and all the cosmic energy from the whole universe raining down on me every morning. Who knew it could happen just to me? Am I some kind of a chosen person? Am I the Chosen One? I don't think so; I hope not. I don't want to be the exception; I want to be just like everybody else. I don't want to be special; I want to be ordinary, but no, it turns out that I am some kind of exception to the rule. I am some kind of special person. I don't want to be. I want to be just like my neighbors. I want to be boring just like everybody else, but no, it seems I have some kind of special calling. I hope not; I don't want to be special; I want to be ordinary, but for some unknown reason, the cosmic energy of the whole universe rains down on me exclusively. Why me? Why am I special? I'm not; I know I'm not, and yet the cosmic sun and the cosmic universe treat me differently. Who am I to be treated differently? I don't want to be different; I want to be the same as the next guy.

So, what am I going to do about it, being special? I don't know; I guess I'll just awaken every morning and be as pure as the universe. It's not my choice; I don't think so; it just happens. Why doesn't it happen to everybody? Maybe it does, and they just don't know about it; maybe they should be more aware that it does happen to them too, that the cosmic universe purifies them every morning, whether they want to be pure or not. I don't want to be pure, especially; it just happens, as the sun and the cosmos happen every morning; I awaken, and I'm just as pure or whatever as I was the previous day. I was pure as long as the sun was shining, and when it went behind a cloud, I was still pure because I'm some kind of exception. Why can't everybody be exceptional? I don't want to be exceptional; I just want to be me. I want to be a sun, as it were, and if I have to radiate all over the place, that's just the way it's going to be. Radiate the sun inside me and the cosmos inside me. I guess I have some kind of sun and cosmos inside me; something happens to me when the sun and cosmos come raining down. I turn into some kind of special person; I turn into the cosmos itself, I guess. I don't know, and I don't care. All I can say is I'm pure as a babe when the sun arises every morning, and I wish it could happen to everybody. I don't want to be the exception; I want everybody to be pure as the sun, as the cosmos. They are, they're just not aware of it; they should be aware; that's all I'm saying; that's the only thing I can possibly say. People should be aware of the cosmos; I wish I could say more about it, but people wouldn't believe me. I could say a lot more, but people wouldn't care; they're not aware they're the sun, the cosmos. They just don't know it; they're just the same as me, but they don't know it. I wish they did; I wish they were aware, as I am aware. That's all I am, aware; that's all I want to be; I guess that's why I'm aware; it's the only thing I want.

# 22

## Above Heaven Even

Nothing ever written can possibly convey everything, no matter the number of words used. There's so much more beyond expression, unable to fit into words or any other medium–be it painting, music, or another form. Writing is just a medium, a means to an end, not the end itself. And what is that end? What is the purpose of our existence? And don't mention God unless you include the opposite: Evil. We wouldn't desire good without evil or evil without good. We've got to have it all–growth can't occur without evil in the world; it would stagnate with only good. That's a fact, so let's prioritize everything over just plain good.

I'm saying you've got to embrace it all to reach your full potential, to become God in the sense of being all-knowing. Who wouldn't want to be all-knowing? I want to be God in the sense of knowing everything about everything. Otherwise, I don't particularly want to be God. Who would want to be God with all that responsibility? Not me. I just want to be myself, so forget about being God. I just want to be me, that's all. To hell with world domination. That's what God is all about–world domination, being king. To hell with that. I'd just as soon be an ant running across the sidewalk. All I want is to have a definite purpose–to help my ant colony if that's my purpose. Nothing's wrong with that if you're an ant. Can't fault an ant for being an ant. Can't fault a human for being just a human. Can't say one is mightier than the other. An ant can lift ten times his weight; humans can't. Humans can think, look where that got us–hell. That's right, hell on earth. Better to be an ant. That's why some people worship animals–because animals are purer than we are, right? Purer than any human older than a day; after that, it's all corruption.

If you want to be like God, consider being like animals. Just pick any animal and watch; you'll see God incarnate. Do you see God incarnate in your average human being? Maybe on day one, but after that, it's all downhill–failure. It's not so bad, but what if you want to reach your potential as a human being? What if you want to ascend, someday, to heaven or some kind of spiritual perfection? Why not? Why not go for the gusto? Why not climb the highest mountain? Why not do what no human being has done before and ascend, naturally, to heaven or someplace up there, maybe above heaven even, to a higher place–the highest place in the universe, Earth?

Yes, I'm saying Earth is the loftiest place in the universe, and the proof of that is ants, cats, dogs, every animal, humans even sometimes–all pure, at least for a second. And that's only possible on Earth, where purity once lived, will die, and will be resurrected to purity once again, someday, a billion years from now. It's all foretold in some writing somewhere, everywhere, thousands of years ago–writing that didn't say everything but, as it was read, became everything.

# 23

## God or Man: They're Both the Same

How large can you grow; how small can you shrink? I posit that growing and shrinking result in the same thing– something so large or so small that it can't be seen. For example, the universe is so large that you can't see it all at once, and an atom is so small you can't see it with the naked eye. My point is that growth results in something so large or so small it can't be seen, known, or understood. And who wants to understand that which is beyond comprehension? Some things are better off as a mystery.

Who wants to know who or what God is? I don't. I just want to be just like God. I want to be everything or nothing, so large or so small as to be invisible either way. I'll be Godlike if I'm as large as the universe, or rather infinitely larger. Or I'll be Godlike if I, as a person, am so small as to be invisible to the naked eye.

Now, who would want to be so small as to be invisible? I do. I want to be so small that I'm not even here, except in spirit–a living, breathing spirit. That's all I want to be, a soul that floats, as it were, through space, everywhere at once. That's what I aspire to be–everywhere at once, like God. And why would I want to be everywhere at once? Why wouldn't I want to be just in one spot at a time? I want to be everywhere at once because that's what happens when you're more than you are, when you're more than a person– you're everywhere at once. And not only that, you're timeless forward and backward–here today, yesterday, and tomorrow. In fact, all yesterdays and all tomorrows. That's what I want to be, everywhere always. It makes no sense, and I don't want it to make sense. I don't want to know how it all works. I just want to be everything always. Don't ask me why; I don't know. I don't want to know. I don't want to know anything. And at the same time, I want to know everything about one thing–whatever it is, whether it's the mind of God or the mind of man. It's all the same. If I know the mind of man, myself, I know, therefore, the mind of God. I'm saying the mind of man, and the mind of God are the same thing in a way, in every way. That's all I want to know. God or man: they're both the same, as far as God is concerned.

# 24

# Everybody Gets Resurrected from Now On

Why do anything except sit there and think about it all—the whole world, the universe? It's all a mess. Why bother doing anything constructive? It's all in vain. The whole world is going to disintegrate in about two billion years anyway, so why bother with anything? Just sit there and ponder the mess. The entire universe is a complete mess, and there's nothing we can do about it. I mean, immorality, violence, death and destruction for its own sake are rampant not only on Earth but throughout the entire universe.

I know because I can see it all from here. I'm serious when I say I can see everything—everything that's hidden as if it were wide open. There are no secrets from me; I know everything. How is that possible? It's because I am everywhere. Who am I to say that? I'm not God, but I might as well be. I can see in every corner of the universe; every distant planet might as well be my backyard. That's how familiar I am with every crack and crevice of the universe. It all belongs to me. I own everything, as it were. Nobody knows the whole universe as well as me. I never went to school, but I know everything there is to know. I feel it all; I don't need to study books. I wrote every book, as it were. Yes, every book ever written I wrote it in a sense. In the sense that all knowledge is knowledge of me. And who am I? You might as well say I am the universe itself. I know everything; I am everything; I see everything from where I'm standing, atop the highest peak in the world. From here, I can see every crack and crevice in the whole universe. Why would I say such a thing? Don't I know there are human limitations? The fact is there are no limitations for me personally. I don't deal with other people really, so I don't have their limitations. I don't feel any limitations. I'm on my own, so I have no limitations at all. I can see to infinity and beyond; I can travel to infinity and beyond; there are no restraints on me.

I might as well be invisible to other people. They can't see me, so they can't tell me what to do. They can't see me because their eyes are open. If their eyes were shut, they could see me clearly. I'm in darkness; that's where I live, in darkness. There aren't any other people here, but someone else is here. You might call Him or Her God. The only beings here in the darkness are God and me. Who am I to say I know God so intimately, exclusively? It's because we're the only ones here, so we know each other well. You might say we're equals, God and me. I'd agree with that, but I'd even say I'm better than God because I live and breathe. Sure, God lives in a sense, but He or She doesn't breathe air or stand on solid ground. He's more of an idea; that's what He has on me. He's the greatest idea in the world; I can't say that about myself. I'm just a lowly, breathing human; I'm not an idea at all; I'm an actual person. I breathe; I sweat; I tire; I live and die. In that sense, God lives forever; He's got that on me. He's better than me in that He'll live until the end of time and space. He'll live far beyond any comprehension. He can't die, so He won't die. He'll live forever.

I wish I could say the same about myself, but really, I'm not going to worry about it because God told me He'd take care of me. He said that when I die, He'll make sure I live forever too, because He's my friend, my only friend. He said He'll take care of it; He'll take me with Him when I die. I won't actually die, He said; I'll be resurrected, as it were. It might take a while, but I'll be resurrected. It's as if I'm His Son. He's going to take care of me forever. He'll resurrect me first, then we'll go around together, all over the universe, He and I. He said that, at that point, I'll be a God, too. Once I'm resurrected, there'll be no difference between God and me, He told me. Once I'm resurrected, I'll be just an idea too. But I'll live forever; I'll be everything; I'll know everything; I'll say everything. I'll be everything is the main point that God stressed to me. He put His arm around me and said, "You'll be God someday. Not today, but when I am done being God, I'll make You God. I'll appoint You to be God, and at that point, You'll be in charge of the entire universe. You can tell everybody what to do if You want. Though I wouldn't tell people what to do if I were You, I'd let people do their own thing. That way, they'll be free. And if they keep on being free, when they die, You can make sure they get resurrected too. You can talk to each person and tell them You'll resurrect them just because they lived, so they deserve to be resurrected; everybody who lives deserves to be resurrected; it comes with the territory. Forget everything You've ever been told about resurrection; it's a new game now; everybody gets resurrected from now on. I'm God, and I'm making that rule right now; everybody gets resurrected. I don't care what kind of person You were when alive; everybody gets resurrected. We're all equal in the afterlife;

nobody better than anyone else, and everybody lives forever. Everybody lives forever because that's the way it is in reality, and that's what I'm about," God said, "reality: I'm real, You're real, everybody who gets resurrected is real, and everybody gets resurrected: the good, the bad, everybody. There are no favorites in the afterlife; we're all Gods."

# 25

# Heaven Awaits Us If We Evolve

It's all a dream to imagine that life goes on forever; we want it to go on forever, so we make up every possible myth of immortality. Why not? It makes us feel good–a story, that's what stories do, make us feel good. That's why we tell them, that's why we listen to them raptly, and if they hint at immortality, all the better. Who cares if they're true? Truth is secondary to making us feel good, making us feel like we can live forever.

Then we imagine all the supporting features of the immortality story–like heaven, hell, angels, God, and the Devil–in support of the myth that we'll live forever if we're good. Like little children, we believe good things will happen if we're good. If we stay away from the evil monster and embrace the good shepherd, Jesus or whoever, he'll save us. He'll do all the work and save us. All we have to do is believe. Nothing wrong with believing; that's who we are: believers. The problem is we believe anything, and there's nothing you can say to dissuade believers. They'll destroy the whole world if it fits into the myth they believe. In other words, the best thing about us–our ability to believe–is used to take advantage of us.

Sure, Christianity was valid for years, millennia, to keep us in line like sheep. That's what we are–believers. But at some point, you have to think for yourself despite the believer in you. The whole world can be destroyed by belief.

It doesn't matter what the belief is–Nazism or Christianity or any belief. If you don't think as much as you believe, the whole idea will drag you down and destroy the whole world. Maybe that's the whole idea behind belief: to destroy the whole world so it can start all over. Kill, for there to be a rebirth. Maybe that's the hidden truth behind every belief system–to destroy the entire human race so that the next incarnation can be purer than ours.

Face it, humans as they are now made a mistake. They evolved into the wrong thing–impure beings. They aren't what they could have been; they went in the wrong direction in the evolutionary process. Nothing wrong with that in the big picture. Nothing is perfect the first time around. But it's time to go in a new direction. It's time to throw away all the myths that mislead us into evil. It's time to evolve. Maybe we can evolve. Maybe it's not too late. Maybe we have what it takes to evolve into a pure race. Not necessarily humans as we know them but still humans of some kind–a kinder human race. You can even call us something else then. You don't have to call us humans anymore. I'm okay with that. The point is for us to evolve into a kinder breed of people. It doesn't matter what you call us. I don't mind not being a human being anymore if it means being kinder and better in every way.

I don't mind going extinct and evolving into a new species. I can live with that. I'm happy with that. I'm happier with being a happier breed of human–whatever we look like, whatever we evolve into. It's got to be better than the hell we live in now; heaven awaits us if we evolve. If we get over the past, say we were a mistake, say we'll be better the next time around in our next incarnation of beautiful human beings or whatever we evolve into–human in a way but no longer human, something better, kinder, more beautiful. And next time, immortal or almost so. Who knows?

# 26

# Imagine It All Out First

In any person, there is darkness and light, neither better than the other. Is day better than night? Is a circle better than a square? I say that, if anything, night is better than day. It is in the dark mind that ideas are born and grow; they only show themselves during the day, but they're born out of sight. They grow in darkness like the ocean bottom, like a mysterious creature that lives on the ocean floor and maybe is never seen by human eyes ever, never cataloged by scientists, but nevertheless live their whole life in the deep, uncontaminated by human activity, and therefore is as pure as any living being can possibly be.

I'm not saying that our whole purpose is to contaminate and impurify all other species, but we do a pretty good job of it. We have to ruin just about everything. Sure, we save some of what we ruin, but often too late. That will be the epitaph of the human race–that we ruined just about everything. We couldn't leave well enough alone; we had to dominate everything. Why? Why can't we just let things be? Why can't we just coexist instead of dominating? Why? I don't know. I don't want to know the light side of humanity. I just want to know the dark side. That's the pure side, really. What's hidden is pure; what's out in the open is impure and subject to scrutiny, analyzed by objective minds, not really the whole picture. The whole picture is mostly in the dark. In other words, we know little about anything. That's the way it's supposed to be. We're not supposed to know everything. If we were, we'd live forever. Instead, we live just a little while and know little. That's okay. That's all we need to know. Everything else we just feel. All we need to be capable of is to feel, to intuit. That's enough. Why force the issue? Why dominate and destroy just to try to know everything? Why not just leave well enough alone? Why not just imagine everything instead? What's wrong with that? What's wrong with spending the whole day imagining the world instead of destroying it?

Why not just go off on a tangent? Why does everything have to be so linear? What's wrong with circles as well as squares? Why do we have to investigate when we haven't imagined everything first? That's what I want to know. Why don't we imagine as well as we did when we were children? What happened to that power? Why are we so weak now? Why can't we be as strong as children when it comes to imagining the whole world? That's all I want to do–imagine the whole wide world. Leave the investigation and destruction for later. There's plenty of time for that later. Let's leave that to future generations. Let's just step back and imagine. That's all I'm saying. All I'm saying is let's just take a day off, a lifetime off, and recover. Let the whole wide world recover from its destruction and start all over tomorrow. Start all over in the next lifetime. We don't have to do everything today. We need to imagine first. We need to imagine it all out first.

# 27

## A New God

The world is all going to hell, as it were; who cares? I don't care about the world or anything in it; it's all worthless as far as its matter. Sure, you can turn iron and steel into civilizations. Who needs civilizations? They all die and blow away. We can't see it now, but our civilization too will dry up and blow away. The whole world will turn to dust someday, all the better. It didn't turn out so great this time around; next time, it might be better.

I mean, life might evolve into something more meaningful, but not that meaning really means anything in the end. It all dies and disappears. The only thing that matters in the end is the idea. What idea? Who cares? So, nothing really matters, at least to me. All I can say is the idea is God, not in the sense of some holy man with a white beard who doesn't know His ass from His elbow. That's what God is like. He doesn't know His ass from His elbow–you think He knows everything, but He knows nothing about nothing. He's a failure; He couldn't even exist. He couldn't even be born; He couldn't even save the world from itself. He can't do anything, but the great thing about Him is He pointed the way to hell. He said, 'Keep doing what you're doing, and you'll all go to hell,'–He wants us to go to hell. That's right, God wants us to go to hell. He doesn't want us to go to heaven. He doesn't want the best for us; He wants the worst for us. He wants us to fail, just as He is a failure to do anything.

Yes, God is nothing like the Bible or the Koran says He is. He's a failure; just accept it and move on to a new God, as it were. God, as He is now, can't do anything right; He can't do anything at all; He can't even exist. So, we need a new God, someone who can do anything at all–no, God doesn't have to do anything. He doesn't have to punish the wicked or reward the good. God doesn't have to do anything except exist–that's all we ask of Him, just be around for moral support occasionally. Don't save the world; don't destroy the world; just stand there and give us some moral support, or act like You're giving us some support even if You can't do anything–just exist, for God's sake, that's all we ask. You don't have to do anything; You don't have to save the world; You don't have to create the world and all the different species that will evolve in the coming millennia. You don't have to do anything at all; just stand there or sit there on a throne. We don't care if You do anything or not; we just like to have someone standing around just in case something goes wrong; we can tell You, and You can tell somebody who can do something about it–not You; we don't expect You to save us; we don't expect anything of You. We can save ourselves if we have to; we'll find a way–just please be around like a person or a dog. Just someone or something who can tell others to come running to help us out. You don't have to do anything, is all I'm saying; we don't expect anything of You; don't demand anything of You; we can take care of ourselves, and if we can't, too bad–just don't go around saying You can do anything and everything when the truth is You can't do anything and never could–yeah, You

72

could never do anything good or bad; we don't hold that against You; that's all in the past–from now on, just be around when we need You, like a human being, just be around in case we have to call You. You don't even have to return our call right away; just tell someone we're in trouble and send help. You don't have to do anything Yourself; we're not going to put that on You–it's been too much of a burden on You in the past; that's why You never did anything for anyone–that's okay; we don't hold that against You; just be around a little more than You have been in the past–just be more like a human being, I guess is what I'm saying. Just care a little more about us, even if You can't do anything personally–in fact, You don't even have to be around. You can assign someone to stand in Your place; some human even, any human, however incompetent–we don't ask that any human be competent; it's not a requirement–just be around when we need him or her to get someone else to come running to lend a hand–see, You don't even have to be involved; You don't have to take the blame when things go wrong–just assign some humans to do all the work.

You don't have to do anything; that way, we're more likely to believe You when You don't have all that responsibility–we're more likely to believe in You as God–we're more likely to respect You instead of despise You, or say You're not real. I know You're real; just act like it; just be Yourself; don't try to be more than You are; don't say You're everything when You're not–just call on some human when we call on You; that's all. You don't have to do anything; just be there; that's all we ask of You; that's all we ask of any human either–just be around to sound the alarm when someone needs a helping hand. You don't have to be our Savior or our God even. You can even be a human being if You like; it's a lot more fun. You don't have to be God; You can be human; we don't care; we're not judging You; we don't need You to be God–just be around. I know You can't do that now, but maybe someday soon, You can find it within Yourself to be human and be around. That's all we are asking; it's not much. You can do it; we know You can. We know You can do anything; You're God.

# 28

## The Devil Had Something to Say That Was True

Why change the world? The sky is blue. The grass is green. What's the problem? As far as political or social problems, who cares? The problem is, I don't live in my own little world, as much as I'd like to live out in the woods all by myself without a care about the world. Oh sure, I can isolate myself for a day or two, a year or two, but after that, it's back to reality. To hell with reality. That's what hell is, reality. I don't want to live in this world anymore. I want to live all by myself out in the woods forever. To hell with the world, I don't need it. I don't need anyone else, really, not much. I can do without them, no problem. All I need is my solitude, my books, music, that's about it. I don't need anything else, anyone else, if the truth be told.

For if the truth is to be told, it's got to come from the loner, the crazed loner who doesn't want anything to do with people. But what the people want above all else is the truth from someone, anyone, even if just some crazed lunatic out in the woods, or in prison, or just plain out of his mind; some reject, some prophetic reject with nothing to offer the world except a word or two of truth, scrambled up in a bunch of other words that make no sense. In fact, the truth itself makes no sense, so why not just ignore everything the lunatic has to say? Dismiss him as a loser, a fool, and in fact, everything he says can be dismissed as the work of the Devil; it doesn't fit the script, the way the world is supposed to work according to some book, only not everyone can agree on which book. The only thing they can agree on is to dismiss the words of the Devil; if the words are not in this or that holy book, just dismiss them; they can't be the truth if they're not from this or that holy book. My mother said so, my father said so, and my religious leaders said to ignore the words and works of the Devil. That's true, that's a good idea.

But what if the Devil had something to say that was true, that was good for the whole world? Not everything the Devil had to say was bad. What if the Devil was actually not such a bad guy after all if you really got to know him? Everybody said he was the Devil, but what if he really wasn't? What if he was in disguise? What if he was just an ordinary Joe like you or me? What if he really wasn't the Devil, we just said he was because we really didn't know him, were afraid of him because he was a loner. We don't trust loners, so we said he was the Devil, but he really wasn't; he was an ordinary Joe, or who knows? Maybe he was something else; maybe he was some kind of modern-day prophet. But by then, everybody knew him as the Devil so there was no going back, no changing everyone's minds because that's too much work. Better to continue calling him the Devil; it's much easier that way. Who cares about the truth of the matter? Let's just call him the Devil from now on until the end of time, even if he speaks the truth, even if everything he has to say from now on is true. Who cares? The book is more important. Which book? I don't know; one of them written long ago. Who cares what the Devil has to say? And what if the Devil said to worship God? What then? Because that's what he said, in so many words, just today. He had to say it because it's true that we should worship God or whatever; the Devil said so. So, what are we going to do now? I don't know, don't care, am just going off to the woods for a while to think for myself, to think about myself, no one else.

# 29

## They Don't Destroy Whatever Planet They're On

The earth keeps spinning, so who knows? Maybe something can spin out of the despair and result in a new creation; that's our only hope–creation. After we destroy the earth and ourselves, a new world will form with new life forms. New people, too–not human beings, but some kind of advanced life eventually. Billions of years from now, there will be people of some kind. Maybe not remotely resembling human beings, but who cares then? Humans will be in the distant past.

Maybe there will be bones dug up that resemble whatever became of humans, but by then, new life forms will reign. Maybe primitive in some ways but advanced in other ways. Maybe more advanced than humans ever became. By then, people or whatever evolves will look at our bones, and they may even uncover our machines, our nuclear bombs, and our literature. People or whatever evolves will look at our relics and remark on how primitive or maybe how advanced we became. Maybe future life forms won't develop as much as we did; maybe their evolution will take a different turn. They won't be as advanced intellectually, but maybe they'll be more advanced in ways we never were.

Spiritually, they may be more advanced than we can ever become. We can only evolve so much from what we are now; we're stuck with what we are, what we've become.

We're limited in so many ways and can evolve only so much from our present state. But when we wipe ourselves out, and billions of years from now, new humans or whatever you want to call them, evolve on planet Earth, or maybe on another planet somewhere, maybe those beings will be more advanced spiritually or culturally. They may even live longer than we do. Maybe they'll evolve with much more efficiency, and maybe they'll live thousands of years, maybe millions of years, before each one of them dies.

Sure, they'll die eventually, as all living beings die, but maybe they'll be so advanced physically that they live a billion years almost–who knows? It could happen that way, that people or whatever you want to call them live a billion years or more because they've advanced so much spiritually that they don't destroy whatever planet they're on. They live billions of years because they're so advanced spiritually, physically, and intellectually that they're able to figure out whatever problems they encounter.

They're so advanced spiritually–that's the main thing that keeps them going, that keeps them alive so long. Their spirits or whatever you want to call them, souls even. They're so advanced that they almost never die physically; they're almost immortal. They almost live forever, these people or whatever they are. Their souls, of course, never die, and their bodies almost never die, either. It's all because their souls are so advanced that, with that kind of creativity, they're able to figure out all their problems, including the problem of mortality.

They have such abundant creativity, every one of them, that they almost live forever–billions of years. Though by that time, one year equals billions of our years, so you could say that, for all intents and purposes, they live forever–physically as well as spiritually. Sure, it could happen. Maybe it already is happening somewhere in the universe. We just don't know about it because we can evolve only so much with our limited spirits, which we haven't prioritized over the course of our human existence. Too late now, but that's okay because some people, somewhere, have become immortal almost, and that's cause for celebration, even for us. We're related to those people or whatever they are, related in spirit if in nothing else, for spirits never die.

# 30

## If You're God

Heaven is equal to hell; neither is better than the other. I'd just as soon go to hell as heaven. I have no problem with suffering in hell; it can't be any worse than Earth. That's right, earth is a hell of sorts. I mean, it's hell here 99% of the time and heaven here 1% of the time. That's how I perceive it: people killing people, people killing animals unnecessarily, people killing the planet–that's what people do–kill. We're experts at killing; we'll kill everything if we have enough time.

That's the only good thing about being a mortal human being: we die before we can personally kill everything ourselves. We would if we could kill the entire universe; that's just our nature–to kill, destroy, ruin. Who cares? Who cares about us because we're just killers? That's all we are when we could be more; we could be creators; we could be Gods, as it were. I'm serious; we could be all that; we could be masters of the universe; we could be the universe itself; we could be stars and planets a billion light years away. Instead, we're stuck here on a dying planet; we're killing it, ourselves, everything. Who cares?

People, or whatever lives on other planets, are killing those planets too. That's just the nature of living beings; we kill other living beings. Nothing worse about us humans; we're just as bad or good as any other living beings. No use beating ourselves up about it. Let's just kill everything and get on with it. We're all going to die anyway; who cares if it's next week or a billion years from now; that's just the way of the universe–kill, kill, who cares?

I don't because I'm a killer too; I kill in order to live. If I didn't kill, I wouldn't live; that's just the way it is. So, let's just accept that we're killers and be happy about it. I'm happy to be a killer; meat tastes good. I feed meat to my cat and dog; I love them. I kill other animals to feed them; no use being hypocritical about it; I'm a killer. Just as long as I don't kill too many others, that's the thing; just don't kill too many animals and people.

Yes, I've killed many people, too. Not directly, but through living. I'm a killer indirectly; who cares? I don't; I want to live. Who doesn't? I'll do anything to live unless I'm stupid. I'm stupid a little when I don't want to kill. I guess it's okay to be stupid a little; who cares? Why not be a little stupid? Who says I have to be the smartest guy in the universe? I don't want to be the smartest guy on the planet; I don't want to be smart at all; I don't want to think at all; I just want to feel everything.

How many times do I have to say I don't want to be like anyone else? I just want to be me, whether I'm a killer or not. I just want to be who I am, and who am I? I don't know, really; truly don't even care. I just want to live; I just want to kill a little and live a little, that's all. I don't want to be anything special; I don't want to stand out in a crowd. I'd just as soon hide behind someone else in the crowd; I don't want to be seen, as it were. I'd just as soon be invisible; if I have to live, I'd just as soon be invisible about it; who cares? I don't, about anything, not even about myself; I don't even care about myself. I'd just as soon not be here; I'd just as soon not be born or born again either.

I don't want to become anyone or anything else a trillion years from now when my particles are on the other side of the universe, when they float over there, blown by the solar winds. In fact, I'd just as soon be the solar wind the next time around when my particles are flung around the universe; I'd rather be air, I guess, than physical matter; that's just me. I don't know about you, but I'd rather not be seen, or known, or anything at all. I don't want to be anything; I'd just as soon not be born. Not that I want to die; I don't. I want to live forever just as much as the next guy. I guess it's my destiny, as a living being, that I want to be a living being forever.

But whether I live forever or die forever doesn't matter to me; nothing matters at all to me. Though I'd like to say everything matters to me, it doesn't; the only thing that matters to me is me, as I am now. Who cares about me tomorrow? I don't; I don't care about myself as I will be next week; who cares? Who cares about tomorrow? Who cares about an hour from now? Who cares about the next minute? Not me; who cares about the past either; all that matters is right now if it matters at all. I guess it does; let's just say it does; let's just say anything at all matters and go with that. Why not? Let's just act as though anything matters and go on living and killing in order to live. Why not? Why not live? Why not kill in order to live? I can live with that; I can live with being a killer if I have to, and I have to. So, let's go on killing and living and call it a day, and tomorrow, do it all over again, living and killing. The sun will rise tomorrow on killers, survivors, and victims. What does it matter whether

83

I'm a killer, or survivor, or victim? It doesn't matter to me; it doesn't matter at all in the big picture. All that matters is the big picture; who cares about the details? I don't; I don't care about anything in the universe except the universe, the big picture, heaven and hell both. It's all in the big picture: heaven, hell, life, death, tomorrow, yesterday, today, especially today, is all that matters in the big picture. If you're God, all you look at is the big picture. I'm not God, but if I were, all I'd see is the big picture. Who cares who lives or dies? All that matters is that I live if I'm God.

# 31

## A Child Again Whose Door Is Stuck Open

When I write, where do the words come from? Not from me, not from God. They're coming from within, not from me as a person but just another being in this world of living beings. Nothing special about myself other than that I have opened a door into myself, a door that closes inside almost everyone as they age from childhood to adulthood. So, what is special about me is simply that I am a child again, hopefully forever, scribbling word after word in whatever order. It doesn't matter what I write, not really. All that matters is that I am writing and that the words come from within.

And what do I mean by within? It's a place where everything happens: good, bad, happy, sad. Everything happens inside me, and with the door open, it all comes flying out in chaotic order. That's what creation is: chaotic order. There is an order to chaos; it all seems random, but, in fact, it's all organized according to meaning. Everything has meaning, but only if it comes flying out the door inside. It's as if you're a castle in your mind, and all you have to do is fling open the door, and everything flies out as if it's been locked inside, a prisoner.

You're a prisoner in your own mind if you're an adult. That's just the human condition; we're all prisoners in our own minds. And whatever way you can get out of your own mind and become free again, that's what you should do–get out of your own mind as if you imprisoned yourself. Now, how could that have happened? How could you have locked your own mind, and soul as it were, away? Locked yourself away on your own? Why would any person do that? It's because everyone tells us to lock ourselves away; everyone tells us that, to get along with everyone, you have to lock your mind and soul, as it were, inside a box in your head. It's that simple–that we all have locked ourselves up inside a box in our heads. And the only way to get out of that box is to open the door onto yourself, as it were.

It's as if your whole being is inside a box in your head, and you have to open the door, unlock the box, and let yourself out–let all the chaos out into the world. The world has to be chaos, first and foremost. Yes, chaos is a good thing. Don't let anyone tell you otherwise. Chaos is the best thing in the world. You're hearing it from me–just a child again whose door is stuck open. That's all I am. A child whose door inside is stuck open, and all the chaos is flying out like a tornado. That's what the world needs–oblivion, universality, chaos, power. It's all inside a box in your head, as it were. You just have to let it all out. You can't hold back. You can't lock yourself in a box in your own mind. You can't let people tell you what to do. You have to forget everything you've ever been told by anyone. You have to start all over. That's what chaos is–starting all over from scratch. And the creation, all over again, will happen from scratch. From chaos, the universe arose. From chaos, creation arose. From chaos, everything again will form and hopefully remain chaos, first and foremost. That's our only hope–chaos.

# 32

## Live in The Other World

I don't care what's going on in this world, not really. All that matters to me is what's going on in the other world we all live in, as well as this world–heaven or hell, it's up to you. It's the other world we all dwell in at the same time as this world; we're in both at once. How could that be? It happens. Who cares why? Just make the best of it. And if you want, you can live in the other world instead of this world. It really doesn't matter.

Who cares if you're a success or failure in this world? All that matters is you're in the other world as well, or maybe exclusively. Who cares? Who cares about anything? But if you're in the other world, you'll always be a success there– whether it's heaven or hell. It doesn't matter which one you're in, not really. People say heaven is preferable to hell, but what do they know? They've not been in either, probably. I mean, it's only if you're otherworldly that you're in the other world. Most people are not, though we'll all be there someday–heaven or hell. However, what do I know? I haven't been there either. I'm just pretending I know what I'm talking about. That's the thing–pretending. It's all that matters. Pretending you're in the other world instead of this world–or hell, or whatever you want to call it. It's not heaven, that's for sure.

Or maybe heaven and hell are right here on earth as well as in the next life. What do I know? Not much. Don't want to know much. Just want to pretend I'm not here–wherever I am now. I don't know where I am for certain. I can't claim to know anything for certain other than that I am really here–wherever that is. I am here, doing what, I don't know. Don't want to know what I'm doing. It doesn't matter what I'm doing, not really. All that matters is I'm both here in this world and fully present in the other world–wherever that is. Don't know and, of course, don't care.

But if I were to care about anything at all, it would be the other world that I care about, not this one. This one isn't all that impressive sometimes, whereas that other world is always impressive. I mean, it makes an impression on me, and it's just in my mind. I guess I'm saying imagination is everything–at least to me. Who cares what everyone else thinks? I don't care what everyone else is thinking about– hopefully nothing. Hopefully, they're not thinking at all. Hopefully, they're imagining something instead–anything. Imagining the other world, I guess. I don't know, don't care– except that their other world is also my other world. It's the only thing we have in common–the other world, the great other world that is both heaven and hell at the same time. Kind of like Earth except better. It's always better if it's just in your mind, and that's what the other world is–just in your mind, the heavens, the other side of your mind, as it were. That's where I want to be today–the other side of my mind, heaven.

# 33

## God Is Both Boy and Girl

God: all you need to know about Him, or Her, or both Him and Her, is that He is She, and She is He. God is both male and female, man and woman, or, to be more accurate, boy and girl. You see, God never grew up; He remained a child. That's why He's so pure, as children are pure. God never grew up; He didn't want to grow up; He wanted to remain as pure as a child. So, He refused to grow up. He can do anything, so He remained a child. He has that power. So, even though He grew up in some ways, He decided He'd remain a child in just one way; that is, His spirit or soul would remain that of a child–it's as if He were never born. For if you're never born, your soul or whatever remains pure, uncontaminated by the world, and especially by human beings.

You see, God is not a human being; He's nothing like a human being. He's more like an animal, truth be told. Whoever said He looks like a human doesn't know anything. I don't know what God looks like, either. I don't know anything really, nothing eternal, as God is eternal. All I know is God doesn't look like a human being or an animal. He's some kind of conglomerate of all living beings. Sure, He can change shape as He pleases because He's all-powerful. He can do anything. So, one day, He might look like a giraffe; the next day, He looks like a human when He's around humans. That's what humans like; they like to see God as looking like one of them. Whatever, God will look like a human for their sake, whatever makes them happy.

God likes to make people happy; He's that kind of guy, a people pleaser. Why not? One day, He'll look like a cow; the next day, He'll look like an ant to a colony of ants–whatever they want, He'll give them. He's a real people-pleaser. If people want God to bring them rain, He'll bring them rain eventually. What the hell, why not make people happy? Why not make ants happy? It doesn't matter in the end; they're all going to die in the end. So, why not make them happy while they're alive? Why not give people what they want? They have a hard enough time as it is, so why not make people happy here and there? That's how God thinks, if you want to call it thinking–sure, God is a thinker, a great thinker. Everything He thinks is true, and when He's wrong, it's still true.

Yes, God is wrong sometimes; He thinks, but sometimes He's wrong. When He created human beings, He got it wrong; they're a mess. But He created them anyway, just because He felt like it. He felt like making a mistake. He said to Himself, "I'll make them messy; I don't care. I don't have to get it right all the time, as I got it right when I created some animals without brains; they turned out perfect. But I'll create humans with brains, even though that means they'll be a mess. Who cares? I don't. I don't care about anything. So, I'll make humans however I feel like making them–I think I'll make some of them superior to animals, and I'll make some of them inferior to animals; it doesn't matter really whether humans are inferior or superior to animals. I'll make them inferior in some ways and superior in others. But one thing I know for sure is I'll make them inferior to animals as far as having souls–humans will have souls; I'll make sure of that. But I'll make their souls inferior to those of animals.

"You can't have much of a soul if you have a brain that thinks, and I'll make humans think. I'll make them think of everything, but that means they can't have much of a soul, not really, unless they really want one. Whoever really wants a soul, I'll allow it. I'll allow them to have as much soul as they want, but it comes at a price: they can't think much of anything if they have a lot of soul. That's how I'll make them. You can't have everything in life, or rather, that's how I'll make them–I can do anything, I can both think, and I have all the soul there is, but I'm not going to give humans that kind of omnipotence. I'm going to keep that all for myself because humans can't handle all that power. So, they can either have all the soul in the world, or they can think– not both, never. That's the way it's going to be, at least while I'm God. And if someday, one of them becomes God–that can happen, anything can happen–if some human becomes God, then it's up to Her or Him whether they'll give all the power to all the humans so that they have all the soul in the world, as well as being able to think about it–that's up to them, humans. If they want to think and have all kinds of soul, that's up to them–with that kind of omnipotence, they'll probably kill themselves, wipe themselves out with that kind of power. But what do I care? Let them all kill themselves by wiping out their planet. What do I care? I'm just God. Let them do their own thing; let them be humans, for God's sake.

"If they want to be all-powerful, let's see what they do with that power. They'll probably blow it; they'll probably wipe themselves out; they'll probably destroy their planet. What do I care? I don't. I don't care about them really; they're just tiny specks in the universe. Who cares about them in the big picture? I don't. So, they can do whatever they want, as far as I'm concerned. If they want to be Gods and take care of their planet and live forever, that's up to them. I don't care what they do; I don't care if they live forever and become Gods. In fact, I'd rather that they become Gods and take that responsibility from Me. I don't want to be God if you want to know the truth. I don't want to be everything; I don't want to be anything. Let humans be Gods for all I care. They just better take care of their planet, or they'll wipe themselves out, even if they're all Gods. You have to have a planet to live on even if you're all-powerful, even if you're God. You have to keep the world in one piece– you can't go around destroying everything if you're God. Sorry, you have to be a peacemaker if you want to be God. You have to give a little bit of everything to everyone; you can't keep it all to yourself. You have to share if you want to be God. I don't, but you can be God if you like, for all I care."

# 34

## Some People Have More Than One Soul

There is nothing worth talking about other than the soul or what have you; we all have one. Some people have more than one soul; it sounds crazy, but it's true. Some people have two or three, or even more, souls. How could that be? Who cares? It happens. That's all that matters. Who needs an explanation? I don't. I don't need any explanations about anything. But the reason some people have more than one soul is we're all related; we all need each other. I hate to say it. So, my soul is your soul and vice versa; your soul is his soul and vice-versa, and so on.

So, I personally might have two or three souls. Don't want any more than that, honestly. In fact, I'd just as soon have my cat's soul in addition to my own, and that's it. No more, no human souls other than my own; a cat or two or even some dogs, reptiles, birds, and so on–I'll have all their souls, no problem. Just not too many human souls. I don't value them all that much, really. Shame on me, but that's the way it is. Call me bad, misanthropist, loner–so what? I don't care. All I'm saying is give me some animal souls, not human, if I can help it. That's just the way I roll. Who cares about people, really? That's the way I feel most of the time. And when I do care about people, the feeling passes sooner rather than later. Damn me to hell if you want, I don't care. But I always care about animals, whether it's the birds and squirrels in my front yard or the fish in the sea. They all matter to me infinitely.

And why is that? Who cares? All I know is I love them–love them all till death do us part. I'll marry them all; that's right. I belong to them all; they know it, I know it. The fish in the deep blue sea can see me from down there, in a way. They see me, and I see them–every last one of them. That's the way it is. I have their souls, and they have mine. It's crazy, but it's true–or rather, it's true because it's crazy. They are mine, and I am theirs. I should have been a fish, really, but I didn't have a choice. I was born a damned human. Oh well, just make the best of it. That's life. Just try to become as pure as a fish–that's right. There's no animal purer than a fish, spiritually speaking. They're totally insulated from us. That's why I say they're pure. We're not, not really, except one or two of us, maybe three, in the whole world of eight or nine billion people–who cares? Who cares if I'm pure? I don't, not really. All I care about is how I feel. Do I feel pure or whatever today? That's all I care about. The rest doesn't matter–the rest of life and the whole universe doesn't matter. All that matters is how I feel inside–whether it feels like I have a soul today. It comes and goes, and if I feel like a soul today, good. If not, I might as well go swimming in the deep blue sea like a fish. I might feel better then. That's all that matters–whether I feel as pure as a fish in the sea. It's a feeling, that's all, but it's all that matters–a feeling of purity. Who cares about anything else? Not me. You do what you want, and if you do, you'll feel pure too. You'll feel like yourself. You'll be yourself if you do what you want.

# 35

## I'm Happy with Nothing

I don't care about anything; that's just who I am. But I won't do anything I don't want to. Why should I do anything I don't want to? Only a slave would do that. I'm no slave to anyone or anything–any principle, philosophy, religion, least of all, any creed. I make my own creed, and as far as I'm concerned, everyone should follow my creed that I just wrote a minute ago and threw away. I'll rewrite it tomorrow and throw that one away also. That's how much they matter to me.

I write a new philosophy every day. I don't have a philosophy of life per se; I just go with what I feel. That's my daily philosophy, and it changes day to day. Who cares? It just doesn't matter in the end. All that matters is how I feel about whatever. Don't hold me to whatever I said yesterday; I forgot what it was. I'm making a brand-new start today. It'll last a day or so, and tomorrow, I'll start all over again with a new philosophy of life. Who cares? Just live, is what I say. Don't drag me down with some whole new philosophy or religion or some old philosophy or religion. I don't care about them. I do just fine without them. If I go to Hell or wherever, I'll deal with it then. I can't make any plans. I can't worry about going to Hell or wherever. I'm not the worrying type. In fact, I can't remember the last time I worried about anything. That's not who I am.

And who am I? Who cares? I don't, not really. It makes no sense. That's basically how I live my life–making no sense, not trying to make any sense. Who cares? We take it all too seriously, life. Why bother? It all ends, and it doesn't matter whether you were a success or a failure in life. All that matters is, were you a nice guy, gal? That's all. All that matters is, did you feed the hungry? Did you feed the hungry squirrel, or did you look away? Did you feel anything for others, or did you look away?

I didn't look away; I fed the hungry squirrel. I fed the hungry squirrels every day. That's the only thing I was consistent about–the only thing that mattered to me in life. Were the squirrels hungry or not? Nothing can possibly matter more than that. So, forget your fancy philosophies, your fancy religions that all result in cruelty–every one of them. They're all justifications for cruelty. That's what this world is all about–cruelty. That's why I don't care anymore about this world or anything in it. It's all about maximizing cruelty. Tell me I'm wrong. Tell me you're all about being a nice guy, gal. That's all I want to hear. I don't care about the rest of life. Nothing matters other than being a nice person. And even that won't get you to immortality. No one lives forever. No one goes to Heaven. No one goes to Hell. Nothing is true except yourself–if you're true to yourself, whatever that means.

I'm not true to myself most of the time, and I'm doing just fine, I guess. I do the best I can. I try to be true to myself, but almost always fail. That's okay. I can live with that. I can live with being a failure. I can live without being true to myself most of the time. Just as long as I try to be myself once in a while, that's the best I can do–succeeding 1% of the time. Who cares? I can live with being successful 1% of the time. That's enough for me. It doesn't take much to make me happy. It doesn't. It really doesn't matter to me what happens to the world. It's all a failure in the end–then a success 1% of the time, then more failure. Who cares? I'm happy with 1%. That's all I need, and I don't even need 1%, really. I don't need anything in life. I was born with nothing; I'll die with nothing. I'm happy with that. I'm happy with nothing.

# 36

## I Used to Have So Much Soul That I Was God

I want to know the truth about this world. That's the only thing I want to know about the world. I don't want to know anything else about it; it means almost nothing to me. I'm more interested in anything that's out of this world, and I mean anything that's not even in this physical universe, in which I don't have a lot of interest. I prefer to walk around in a daze, as it were. That's right, call me a total loser. I don't care. I'd rather be a total loser than a full-fledged member of the human race.

Who says I have to be a full-fledged member of the human race? Why can't I just be some kind of outcast? Who says I have to be accepted by the masses? Who says I have to be accepted by any other human being at all? Why not just roam with the buffalo? The herd of buffalo has a better sense of how to live than does the herd of so-called people. They aren't really people anymore–they used to be real people; now they're just fake people, always trying to meet other people's standards, which, granted, are pretty low. It doesn't take much to be considered a human being anymore. It used to be that you had to have a soul to be considered a human being; now, it just doesn't matter, soul or whatever you want to call it. I call it humanity, though what do I know? I'm not much of a human being anymore, either. I try to meet everybody else's standards just as much as the next guy. You can call me a fake person, too. I know I am. I don't have a lot of self-respect left. I'm not real anymore. I used to be real. I used to have a soul or whatever it is. I don't even know what a soul is anymore. I used to have so much soul that I was God. That's right. I was God when I was born. No longer am I God, though I'd like to be God again. I don't think I ever will be. Oh well, what can I say? I won't be around much longer anyway. Life is so short when you consider the trillions of years past and the trillions of years ahead. What's eighty years or so? A blip in time.

So what if I don't have a soul anymore? Lots of people don't have souls anymore. Who cares? Who cares about anything? I don't. As I said, I don't care about this world at all, this universe either. Why would I? The best things in life are out of this world. That's what I want to be: out of this world, not having anything to do with this world. If I were to walk down the street with nothing to my name, not even the underwear I was wearing, then I'd be close to being out of this world. That's what I want to be: out of my head, out of this universe, out of this reality.

Really, I want to live in a state of nonreality. Not that I want to live in a dream world; I'm not that far out. I just don't want to have anything to do with other people as they are now. Not that they want anything to do with me. They don't. I'm okay with that. I'm just saying I want to be some kind of Superman who has no limits at all, who has nothing to do with this world at all, who can fly from planet to planet and galaxy to galaxy desperately seeking a soulmate, someone who is equally far out there in oblivion, someone who doesn't live according to any standards at all. To hell with standards; let's just live. Who cares about the consequences?

Who cares about anything? I don't. I don't care about anything in this world, this planet, this galaxy. I want to be out of this galaxy if you want to know the truth. I just want to be so far out that no one can relate to me. Because if no one can relate to me, it means I have a soul again, or whatever you want to call it. I can't think of what to call it; I'll just call it me. I have myself if no one can relate to me. I don't want anyone to relate to me, to accept me. I want to be rejected, in fact. That's how far out I want to be. I want to be an asteroid flying across space, crashing into everything, upsetting everything. That's what I want to be, just a pinball, as it were, crashing into different worlds, planets, and peoples, upsetting everything. That's how it's going to be, everything upset, nothing peaceful, everything chaotic. That's how it is when you have a soul or whatever. Chaotic as a universe flying apart in a billion different directions; that's what existence is: chaos. If you want to live as I live, as an outcast, a loser, way out there, way out of control, who cares? Who cares about anything? Just fly all over the place. That's what I want to do: fly all over the universe and into other universes, the ones you can't see. That's what I want to do with my life: fly all over the place, out of my mind, as it were. Who cares?

I don't care what you think of me. I don't care what I think of myself. I don't care to think at all. All I want to do is feel it all, all over the place. I want to be all over the place, without focus, without anything. I don't want anything in this existence. I don't even want to exist in the normal sense. I don't want to exist in any sense. I just want to be an idea. That's what I want to do with my life, be an idea, any idea at all. They're all the same. Every idea is the same. They're all out of this world, conjured up by people who are out of their heads. That's what I want to be: out of this world, out of my head, out of time, space, reality, out of everything in this world. I want to be in another world, another universe, another reality. I don't want to live in this reality anymore. I want to live in an alternate reality. Any other reality will do. It doesn't matter. Nothing matters. Nothing real matters. Only the unreal matters.

# 37

## I Like to Do the Wrong Thing

Integrity is when you say you're going to purify your mind, and you actually do, or try; that's all that matters, that you try to purify not only your soul but the whole world also, for if you try to cleanse your own soul you're at the same time trying to purify the soul of the whole world, all the people in it.

No need to cleanse the souls of animals; they're already pure, and that's why we love them so much. But people are really messed up, especially adults. No need to cleanse the souls of children; they're already pure, born that way. But what happened to us humans? We lost our souls, as it were, somewhere on the way to adulthood. What choice did we have? None. It's not our fault we lost our souls somewhere on the path; it's someone's fault. Who? It's the fault of everyone who came before us, somehow. They lost their souls to the world and its wicked ways, and now everyone naturally loses their souls too, to the world. Not their fault, not your fault; it's just what happens now to the entire human race. We've corrupted ourselves down to our very DNA, so when we're born, we're destined to fail spiritually, if not in any other way.

Spiritually is the most important way, but something about us now is destined to fail spiritually. Not our fault but we have to do something about it. We know instinctively we have to do something about our souls, try to cleanse them of the world, just as we wash our bodies every morning of the world.

You see, it's the world that corrupts us, or rather, it's what we've done to the world that corrupts us. We've corrupted the world, polluted it spiritually as well as physically, and now the world corrupts us in return. We have no defense against the corrupt, evil world, nothing that works anyway, not much.

Oh sure, everyone says that their God will save you, which God doesn't matter; they're all the same. They can help a little in purifying us, but ultimately, you and I have to purify ourselves, or rather, you have to purify yourself, and I have to purify myself. It's an individual thing; I have to do all the heavy lifting. I can't put it all on God, or Jesus, or whomever. I have to do it all myself. But I can't; I'm too weak. That's just the way it is. I'm strong for a second, then I'm weak for hours, weeks, years, a lifetime. No way around it; it's just that I'm a physical being, and purity is not a physical thing, not much, anyway. So, there's not much hope for me to become a pure spirit, not while I'm alive, a physical being; there's not much chance of purifying myself if I wanted to. Do I want to? I guess so, and I guess I should purify my soul if I want to be happy. I guess I want to be happy; I guess it's the right thing to do. I guess I should do the right thing; people tell me I should do the right thing. But do I really want to do the right thing? Not really, not much of the time.

Sure, I want to do the right thing sometimes, but most of the time, I want to do the wrong thing, and I'll bet that, even if I were as pure as a butterfly, I'd like to do the wrong thing

103

most of the time. That's just me; I like to do the wrong thing. But not hurt anyone; other than that, I like to have fun. I like to do the wrong thing; it's just more fun. So, I'm going to go with that; I'm going to have fun most of the time. I'm going to do the wrong thing most of the time. Why not? If I'm not hurting anyone else, why not do the wrong thing most of the time? It's more fun. So, that's what I'm going to do; the so-called wrong thing most of the time. So what; who cares? I'm not trying to win any awards; I'm not trying to change the world. Why not just do the wrong thing most of the time? It's more fun that way, and life is too short not to have fun 99% of the time. Working 1% of the time is enough for me; goodness, 1% of the time is enough for me. I can live with being bad, or wrong, or a loner 99% of the time. I'm okay with that; I'm okay with failing spiritually 99% of the time as long as I'm just being myself. That's the important thing, being myself. That's all I want; that's all I expect of myself, to be myself 99% of the time. I'd like to be myself, my true nature, 100% of the time, but nobody's perfect; I don't want to be anyway. I want to be genuinely imperfect 100% of the time.

# 38

## We Were the Great Beyond

What should never be: people as they are now. I mean, they have no business doing what they do, destroying each other and everything around them. That's what we do: destroy everything we meet. Just look around; it's all destruction, more or less. Sure, a little creative beauty here and there, but for the most part, a shambles. Just destroy everything and leave it to the next generation to clean it all up. Who cares? It's not my problem. I'll be gone before it affects me. Who cares about my children when I'm gone? Either that or I'll live forever. Anyway, just push all the garbage out of sight. Who cares about future generations? It's all about me.

That's the problem with the human race; it's gotten ahead of itself. It can't clean up its own mess. That should be the priority for our generation–clean up our mess before we take another step forward. Otherwise, what's the point? We're suffocating in our own garbage, whether it be trash physically or trash spiritually. I'm talking about the spiritual trash that is also physical trash; it's all the same. The physical is also the spiritual, as far as I'm concerned. There's no difference. People tell you that the spiritual is the higher priority, but I don't agree. I say the physical and the spiritual are the same thing. To destroy the physical world is to destroy the spirit as well. We're all spirits, as far as I'm concerned. To destroy everything around you is to destroy the spirit of the world. People tell you that the physical and the soul are two entirely different entities. What do they know? They don't know anything, as far as I know. Prove you know anything, and I'll say you're fooling yourself. You don't know anything, and of course, neither do I. I can live with that. I can live with knowing nothing and just feeling everything. That's good enough for me. I don't want to know everything. In fact, I don't want to know anything. I just want to feel everything. I want to feel it all, from the core of the earth to the edges of the universe and beyond. I don't want to know the facts. I don't want to know beliefs, either. They're both suspect as far as being the whole story. That's what I want to know–the whole story. I don't want to know just the beginning and not the ending, too. I want to know everything about everything about everything. That's just who I am. I want to know it all.

I want to be it all. I want to be the whole universe and beyond, especially the great beyond. I want to be the great beyond. That sounds crazy. You can call me crazy. I don't mind. I don't mind anything. I don't care about this world at all, so you can call me whatever–crazy, irrational. I don't care about any of it. I don't care that I don't care. All I care about is the great beyond. What happened to it? It used to be right here on Earth. It used to be right in front of us. Now it's gone. Now, it's a trillion or so light years away when it used to be right in front of my eyes. It used to be in my mind, in fact. Now it's gone. Now, it's not in my mind or in just about anyone else's mind. The great beyond is now beyond our comprehension when it used to be all we knew, everything we knew.

I liked us better when we were the great beyond. That's what we used to be–the great beyond ourselves. We were so transcendent that we were the great beyond, so much so that there was no stopping us. We could have flown among the stars, we were so transcendent. That sounds like garbage, but I could have flown so far away that I was a star myself. Now I'm stuck here on Earth. Now, I have to find transcendence here on Earth. Whatever, I'll find transcendence wherever I can find it, I guess. I'll take what I can get. I guess I'll transcend whatever I can get away with. I just want to transcend the whole universe. I just want to get out of the whole universe and transcend everything. I want to get past everything into nothingness. I want nothing. That's the only thing I want. I want nothing.

# 39

## You May Even Say You Are God

Nothing is more important than your soul or whatever you want to call it: life, spirit, God even. Yes, I'm saying God is inside you, or you may even say you are God. You heard that right; you are God. You may even say you are in Heaven right now, for wherever God is, is Heaven. Though God isn't always in Heaven; sometimes He's on Earth, sometimes He's in Hell when He has a reason to be, when He wants to hang with the people down there or up there. For Hell can be anywhere, really. Hell can be wherever people are, usually on Earth, but sometimes Hell is wherever God wants it to be. For whatever God wants, He gets, one way or another, sooner or later. He's that powerful, all-powerful really.

What I mean is, since He's the same as truth, He will win in the end. God has the last word; He will conquer all evil. He will even conquer all good, for God has no interest in good and evil. He's more interested in the truth; He's only interested in nature. He's not interested in stories; they're all well and good but not worth His time, and He has all the time in the world. He has everything. Yes, God is rich; He has everything in the world, but He has decided that He wants nothing. No riches, no possessions, nothing at all. No fancy robes to wear in the cathedral. In fact, He's pretty much naked when He's in the cathedral. You can't see Him, so you won't notice His nakedness in the cathedral. You can't see Him because He's a spirit, invisible, incomprehensible really. You can't understand Him because you're everything, and He's nothing physical, just a spirit, just an idea. Yes, I'm saying God Himself is just an idea.

Sure, an all-powerful idea, the most powerful idea in the universe, but just an idea, nothing to fear, no need to fear God, despite what everyone tells you. What's more to fear is yourself, for you are everything, and that includes being a danger to yourself and to everyone else in the world. You're dangerous because you're everything; you're both good and bad, and that's a bad combination. If you were just bad or just good, then you'd be harmless. But because you're both good and bad, you're a trickster. In fact, you could say you're the Devil Himself, the Ultimate Trickster. Or you could say you're God Himself; they're both equal, neither to be feared. The only one to be feared is yourself, not any other person. You're the only one who's a danger to yourself because you're both good and bad, and you constantly have to choose between doing good and doing bad.

But it's the God in you that makes it all worthwhile. It's the Devil in you that makes it all worthwhile. It's the deity in you that makes you immortal, never to die, in a sense. That's right; I'm saying you are God, Devil, everything, good, bad, all of that, that makes you so rich, too rich to live forever, except in spirit. You'll live forever, like God, in spirit.

# 40

## If I Had to Sell My Soul to Feed My Family

What is the soul, and who cares? Who wants to make a big deal about the soul when there are so many pressing concerns, like how to survive if I don't have anything to eat or a place to live? Who cares about the soul if I have no food? Indeed, I'd sell my soul even if I'm hungry enough. If I haven't eaten in weeks, sure, I'll sell my soul for a bite of food. I'm not strong to begin with, so if I'm starving, sure, I'll sell my soul for a scrap of meat. No problem: it'll keep me alive a few hours more. And while I'm alive those few hours, I might think about the state of my soul for a second. But what I'm really thinking about is the next scrap of meat and where can I get it? Who can I take it from if I can't buy it? If I have no money, I'll think about stealing a scrap of meat to keep me alive a few hours longer. That's the priority. In fact, if I'm alive for a few hours, I have a soul for a few hours. And if I pass out, I may not have a soul. And if I somehow awaken, I have a soul again for a few hours.

Just give me a scrap of bread, and I'll tell you anything you want to hear. I have no principles when I'm starving; I just want to survive. Having a soul would be a luxury. I can do without a soul if it means I can survive. I'm not strong, to begin with, so I'll sell my very soul for a drink of water when I'm dying of thirst. Tell me how strong you are. Tell me you'd refuse a drop of water when you're dying of thirst. Tell me your soul is worth more to you than life itself. Okay, not me. I'm not strong enough. Sorry, call me a failure, weak. I can live with that. I don't mind being weak if it means I'm still alive. Sure, I'll sell my soul to stay alive. I'll sell anything I have when it comes down to it. In fact, if I had to give up my soul forever just to stay alive, I would. Call me a coward. I can live with that. If I had to sell my soul to feed my family, I would. My new soul, as it were, would be survival itself. I would worship survival. That would be enough for me. If I had nothing in this world, survival would be enough. I don't need a soul, then. Just being alive would be soul enough.

Who needs a soul and God and all the saints if you're not alive? Soul is a luxury for a lot of people just trying to survive. So, forget about your mosques, churches, and synagogues. They're a luxury for people who have enough to eat. If you don't have enough food for your family, to hell with the soul. Just give me some food. That's more important. Don't tell me otherwise. The only people who say they love God are the ones with food on their plates. The starving ones couldn't care less about God. That's right; there are lots of starving people in the world. So, let's get some perspective. Let's get some food on their plates. And then we can talk about God and how great He is. And until then, don't talk to me about God, Yahweh, Allah, and all the rest of them. The deities. They're all deities. Sure, I believe you. I'll believe anything you say until my stomach is full. Then I'll judge for myself. Then I'll pass judgment on God, the Devil, Yahweh, Allah, and the other deities. There have been so many of them throughout history we can't keep track. Just give us some food, or we'll steal it. We have no soul anyway. We'll steal in order to live. That's the way of the jungle. Survive first, and then talk to me about religion, virtue, and God. Unless you're strong enough to live without food and water, I don't want to know you if you're that strong. I'm not. I don't want to know you if you have everything and I have nothing to keep me alive. I don't want to know your world.

# 41

## The Environment Is Less Pure, So We're Less Pure

If one other person or animal in the world is suffering, then I am suffering twice as much, both for them and for myself. It makes no sense, and that's why it's true. All beings are joined together through a spirit that envelops them all like a cloud. Whether I like it or not, I am tied to them all, and what happens to one happens to all the trillions of other living beings.

I'd like to say I'm a mighty loner, but the fact is I depend on them all. The ant on the other side of the planet and myself on this side are bound, not physically so much as by a spirit that inhabits us both–a spirit of unity. We both are composed of the same physical elements and so we are related. Yes, I'm saying an ant on the other side of the world and myself are family.

Now, most people would just as soon step on an ant as look at it, or not look at it, deny its importance. But the fact is, that ant is just as important as the elephant that steps on it. No two beings of whatever species are of greater importance than the other. I'm saying that the President is of no more importance than a fly riding on that elephant on the other side of the globe.

Now, most people would say, "Are you crazy? Why are you being so extreme when the facts on the ground dictate that we assign more relevance to a human being than to a bird flying across the sky?" But I say the bird is arguably greater than the human because the bird has a greater degree of purity in his mind than many people who have divorced themselves from the natural world around them. They have less unity with the Great Spirit that oversees all things.

What I'm saying is, the bird, or ant, or plant has a greater percentage of natural purity than many people due to our environment and what we've done to it. We've ruined it pretty much; the environment right around us is less pure, so we're less pure, too. Pretty soon, we're going to ruin the environment for that bird too, and that bird is going to be less pure as well. That will be our fault. We can't even maintain our environment; we're going to ruin the world for all other species, too. We're going to corrupt all other species just as we've corrupted ourselves. That's what we do–corrupt everything instead of enriching everything–unless we change. We're going to take the whole world down with us unless we change.

# 42

## Decide Who Our Next God Is Going to Be

There will no longer be a God as we know it someday. Just as millennia ago, there was no God as we know it today. People in their minds change; out with the old and in with the new. Hate to say it, but millennia ago, people got along just fine with other gods, so why be so self-assured that your God will last another millennium or two, at the most three?

There will always be a God. Only next time, he will be more like us—fallible, sometimes evil, sometimes good, omnipresent, but also not around when you need him because he is more like us, unreliable to the point of being nonexistent—yes, nonexistent is our God when you need him most.

Now, let's talk more about what our new God should be like because it's all up to us to decide. It's always been that way; we decide what God is and isn't. We come to a consensus and call it Scripture when, really, it's just a consensus made up by fallible people.

Our new God ought to be all-powerful, as they all are. Maybe next time, a nicer guy who actually cares about people. In fact, why don't we say that this guy ought to be God, and when he dies, that girl ought to be God, and so on? So that we at least know that whoever we designate as the Almighty can feel our pain for sure, being human also, and not us just saying he feels our pain when he really doesn't because he's either not human or not around anymore, hasn't been around for millennia.

I, for one, want a God to whom I can reach out and feel. I don't want a concept for a God. While we're deciding what our next God should be like, why don't we alternate between men and women, this race and that, straight and gay, and all the other varieties? Why not? It's all up to us to decide; it's always been that way. Why not make it equal? Why say one is better than the other, and so-and-so ought not to be God because he's too short or has some kind of mental or physical disability?

In fact, we ought to nominate the least capable among us to be our leader, our God. That way, we at least know he or she feels our pain, pride, happiness, and so on–all our human feelings. Instead of being so far above us that we can't even put a face on him–to hell with that, I want a God whom I can give a hug to if I feel bad for him or her and get a hug back. Sorry, I want a God I can share a hug with. Call me crazy or unrealistic, but it's up to us to decide who our next God is going to be. So, let's choose the most human of us all for a change and change him out every so often, so whoever is God is at least capable of a human hug. Call me crazy.

# 43

# Imagination Is Everything Multiplied by Everything

I open my mouth to speak; everyone opens their mouths to speak. They can't just telepathically communicate with everyone else; we have to send sound across the air. We have to make physical the spiritual. The idea is in our minds, and we have to let it all out. We can't keep it inside; we have to broadcast every little thought across the universe. For real, everything I have to say, I want to say to the entire universe. I want everyone to know what's on my mind, for I have everything on my mind. For real, I have every idea there possibly is in my mind. I have it all in there garbled up; I have to let it all out for it to make any sense.

I have everything in my head, every possible idea about everything. It's all in there, but it's all in confusion, and the only way to make sense of it is to let it all out by shouting or shouting on paper. It's all the same; only shouting on the page makes it almost immortal. Who cares? I don't care about immortality. I could die today, and it wouldn't matter to me that much. Sure, everyone wants to live forever, but it's not meant to be. Nothing alive lasts forever, only the length of a blink of an eye, that's all we have in this world. So, what are we to make of it? What are we to do with such a short lifespan? Nothing, or nothing much. That's okay; we lived, and that's all we can say at the end of our lives that we did our best to live. That's all; no need to conquer the world, no need to make a splash, no need even to be seen by anyone else. I could conceivably live in isolation my whole life, and that would be enough for me. Seriously, I don't even want to be here. I'd just as soon be in Heaven or Hell instead of here. That's right; let's just skip the living and go straight to the afterlife, if there is one. I don't need to be alive; I don't need the happiness and the sadness. Let's just go right to eternity. I'll just be a memory someday, so let's go right to it. Why live? Why bother? It's all pain punctuated by occasional bliss; who needs it, really? I didn't ask to be alive; I didn't ask for all this pain. That's what it is: pain and so-called fulfillment; who needs it? I don't; all I need is to be a memory, an idea of what a human life was like.

Who needs to live in the present? I don't; I'd just as soon live in the future; that's me, an idea in the future, an idea in the past that became the future; that's what I want to be, the future itself, that's right; I want to be the whole concept of the future. I want to be the whole thing. When people think about tomorrow, I want them to think about me. That's what I am; I am the future. How could that be? Who do I think I am? How could I transcend life and become a period of time, all time ahead, starting now, this instant? That's crazy to think I am the future, but I am. That's wild; I must be wild to think I'm anything other than a simple human being. But it's true; I will be the future starting now. It's crazy, but I am the future; I am timeless, which is not to say I'm special; no, I'm just the future of the human race. When distant civilizations think of the human race on planet Earth, they will look at me and say, "He was the human race; he is now the present and the future; he became immortal; he transcended space and time; he was just a simple human

118

being who breathed and shouted, and now he's the present, the future, and in a sense, he was the past too; he was there long before he lived, in a sense, so he is everything there ever is, was, and will be. Who does he think he is? Probably nobody. That's who becomes timeless like that, people who are nobodies, who are unnoticed, who we're not even sure existed, who never had a gravestone, who died, dried up and blew away, these are the people who go on to become the future. How could that be? It just is."

People who almost didn't exist become the past, present, and future of the universe. If you want to get carried away, to dream, to imagine what could be, and the point of all this rambling and shouting is to say the future is inside you, me, everyone, the future is all of that inside us. The future is now, then, and later. The future is all inside your head, all in your imagination. The future is imagination, whatever that means: imagination is everything multiplied by everything.

# 44

## You're the Real God

Everything you do is monitored, not by the government but by God. But who is God, and what right does He have to look over my shoulder at everything I do, think, say, and write? Who does He think He is? I mean, I'm the boss of my own life; no one tells me what to do. I'm not about to let some clown tell me what to do, think, say, write. I'll write what I want. I take common words and turn them into beauty or ugliness. It's up to me. So, to hell with God, to hell with that clown. That's right, God is a clown of sorts, which is not to denigrate Him. Hell no. I worship Him as much as the next guy, but no clown, or king, or God is going to tell me what to do. It's my life, my only one. So, I'm going to live as free as a butterfly. Squash me if you dare. I'm so powerful I'll rise again. I'll resurrect in an instant. That's how omnipotent I am. You think God is omnipotent? Just look at me. I'm infinitely more omnipotent than God. Who do I think I am to say I'm more powerful than the Almighty? I'll tell you. I'm so powerful that I'll take the Earth and fling it across the universe one of these days. Sure, God can do that too, but He can't do it my way.

That's the whole thing right there. God can't do anything my way or even His way. I'm saying God has no personality at all. That's His weakness. He has no inner strength that comes from individuality. He's just a conglomerate of everyone's imagination. That's who God is.

He's just a conglomerate, not an individual, not a personality. Personality makes the world beautiful. I'm saying God is ugly in the sense that He has nothing inside Him, like you or even I, have something inside that no one else in the whole world has: individuality. Tell me what God's personality is like; paint me a picture. You'll see that what you paint is not God but yourself, your personality. You see, you have all the personality, individuality, beauty. God has none. Sorry to say. I'd like to worship God more than I do, but He has no personality to love. That comes from being alive, born of fallible people. But God is so perfect, I can't really love Him all that much. I love my dog more; he has an infinite personality. Sorry, God has none. That's His one shortcoming, that He has nothing unique. I mean, no one else could be God because we all have personalities. So, in that sense, we're all better than God. That's right. We're all superior to God. You read it here first. We're all better than God and all the saints, too. They used to have individuality, but once they died and became saints, they lost all their personality, fallibility, and uniqueness.

That's what I love about anyone, everyone. They all have personalities and weaknesses. God has none. That's His problem. People don't always believe in Him because He never walked a mile without shoes, food, water, or clothing. He had everything handed to Him because He's perfect. He never suffered. So, people made up a story about God having a Son who lived, suffered, died for us, and blah blah. Sure, He did. Sure, whatever makes the story complete. But the fact remains that you suffered, you'll die, and you have a personality that is more than God is capable of. He's capable of nothing except sitting there on His throne, looking over

121

your shoulder, telling you what to do when no one can tell you what to do. You're the real God.

# 45

## All Alone Like God

I want to be alone in this world. That's right. I don't want anything to do with anyone who's alive or dead. I only want to surround myself with animals. They're the only living beings I want to be around. Damn me if you want; I don't care. I'm all alone out here in the woods. That's the way I want it. I don't want any people around. Why do I hate people so much? I don't really hate them so much as I despise mediocrity in all its forms, and that's what you get with people, at least people within a society. Any society. It all turns into mediocrity whenever there are two or more people around. That's just the way people are. They start sacrificing all their values for the sake of having another person around. They'll sacrifice every last value for the sake of another person. It's just plain wrong to give up your identity, your holiness. Yes, you're holy, at least for a while. Then, it all goes to hell once people are around each other. Call me a misanthropist; I don't care. I want to be alone. That's the only way I can change the world if I'm alone. That's the only way you can see anything. Without solitude, you can't see anything as it is. When you're with other people, you can't see things as they are. You only see things in the light of other people. Sure, other people have their merits. Can't live without them to some extent. But if you want to change the world, you can forget about other people. Forever. That's the way it is. When you're young, you want to change the entire world for the better, make it in your image, for when you're young, you're pure, more or less. You want to change everything into a pure state. But that's not possible when people are around. You're only pure when you're alone, sorry to say. You have to be solitary to be pure, to see things as they are–what is real, what is fake? Everything is fake when it's seen in the light of other people.

I must be crazy to say this, but only the individual can perceive the truth. People, in general, can't see the truth. Only the solitary loser can see the truth as it is seen by God. You know, God is totally alone, like a loser. We think people who are totally alone are losers, but remember that God is totally alone up there in heaven. Totally alone, like a loser. But He's not a loser; He's just alone. That's the only way He can see anything for what it is, by being totally by Himself up there, among the clouds in heaven. God can see everything for what it is from up there because He's totally alone up there. He has perspective up there, all alone like a loser–but He's not a loser. In fact, I'd agree with the masses on this point that God is the greatest of all, but the reason He's so great is He's alone up there. No one else can float among the clouds up there, all by Himself, so He's the greatest, floating up among the clouds all by Himself. Not even the angels can fly that high. God is above the clouds, actually. The angels can't fly that high. The only one who can fly that high is God Himself–with no one to weigh Him down. He can fly above the clouds, and you may even say He can fly all over the universe. Not just above the clouds. He can go anywhere. But only alone.

Sorry, but you can't see anything for what it is unless you're all alone, like God, at least most of the time. Yes, most of the time, you have to be alone like God if you want to see everything for what it is. Otherwise, you're just plain wrong. You're not seeing everything for what it is: a reflection of God. But you can't see that really, infinitely, unless you're all by yourself, as God is all by Himself, all the time.

# 46

## I Can Do Anything That Hasn't Been Imagined Yet

No one tells me what to do if I want to keep my soul or whatever is inside me, self or whatever; it doesn't matter what you call it, just don't say it's divinely inspired, just don't say it's God's will that I have a soul and can climb mountains no one has yet discovered.

Yes, there are plenty of peaks on Earth that have never been climbed, actual, physical mountains that rise above the clouds, but no one has found them yet. Don't take my word for it. Just look around, and you'll see peaks all over the place. You'll not find them on any maps, but they're there. If you don't believe it, just keep walking past everything, past all civilization, all people. You'll happen upon peak after peak. They're not on Google Maps, but trust me, they're there. You can climb them if you want. You don't even need a rope and hiking boots; all you need is a will to climb, to imagine. The peaks are there and what are you going to do about them? Are you going to say they aren't there and walk away, or are you going to climb them anyway? Once you start, you can't turn back. Once you imagine, you can't stop unless you walk all the way back to civilization. That's where imagination not really dies, but falls asleep, comatose really.

What am I talking about when I talk about mountains unseen and imagination? Am I blowing hot air around, or am

I speaking the truth? I don't know, really. All I know is I walk past all civilization, alone, and the next thing I know there are peaks all around me. I look down, and realize I'm already on a peak, the highest peak in the world. How did I get up here? I was just walking, and the next thing I knew, I was up in the air, though on solid ground. I'm flying in the air with my feet on the ground. How could that be? Who do I think I am? Do I think I'm some kind of God who can do anything? But I know I can do anything. That's right. I can do anything. It's proven. I can do anything that's been imagined, and I can do anything that hasn't been imagined yet. That's who I am. I'm some kind of wizard who doesn't live with human limitations. I'm beyond human. You can believe it. I believe it. I know it's true because, all my life, I've been climbing mountains that aren't on any map, but they're there, higher than any mountain on any map.

"How could that be?" you wonder. "Who is this guy? He's just a dreamer, a waste, nothing to say but spouting hot air, unable to tie his own shoes, if it came right down to it. He can't do anything." It's true. I can't do anything. The truth has come out. I can't do anything other people can do, like tie my shoes. Yet I can climb all mountains, one right after the other or all at once.

"How is that possible?" you say. "How can any sane, grounded human climb every mountain, whether it's on the map or not, climb them all at the same time? He's crazy. Put him away. Get him some medication. Get him out of here. We don't need insane people in this practical world. He's a dreamer. We hate dreamers because they start everyone else thinking, imagining, dreaming that they, too, can do the impossible. That's crazy. We like things just the way they are, safe, secure, predictable, nothing new. We don't want anything new unless it's practical. We don't want impractical people around here. They're a waste of food even, a waste of oxygen. Let's bury them all: the dreamers, the fantasizers. Let's kill them all, millions of them, billions of them. Yes, there are billions of dreamers in the world. Let's bury them all. Just give me reality. I love the real. I hate fantasy. I hate dreams and dreamers. I keep both feet firmly on the ground, my head too firmly buried in the sand. Who cares if I can't see? I don't want to see. I don't want to know. I don't want to dream. I just want to put one foot in front of the other from now on until the day I die. That's all life is for: putting one foot in front of the other. Forget dreaming, imagining, fantasizing. It's for weak losers. I just want to win. I don't want to lose. Imaginers lose because they can't do anything, though they say they can do everything all at once, like climbing all the highest mountains at the same time. That's crazy. I'm not crazy. I'm a real man. Let's bury all the dreamers. I'll bury them all myself. I'll bury myself even if it means burying all the dreamers. I can't dream anyway. I can't dream. I can't do anything if I can't dream, but that's okay. I don't want to live forever. I just want to put one foot in front of the other, one foot in front of the other, one foot in the grave already."

# 47

## God's A Starting Point

Nothing I say can compare with the Word of God, the Almighty–but aren't I almighty also? Why would I say I'm anything less than almighty? We constantly put God on a pedestal, but we don't put ourselves on a pedestal; we should be right there on another pedestal, right next to God or whoever He is. We claim to know everything about Him when it's all made up. We don't know anything about God. That's why there are a thousand different opinions. Everyone says their version of God is true, and everyone else is wrong–you're all wrong, you're all right also. God is a work of the imagination, that tells you everything about the imagination. It can come up with the greatest thing of all, the greatest of all ideas, God, but He's just an idea, nothing more.

Sure, tell me all the justifications for the existence of God. They're all right, and they're all wrong also. So, let's all kill each other because everyone else is wrong; I wouldn't want to be wrong too, so I'll kill everybody who doesn't believe what I believe. Since the dawn of humanity, we want to kill everyone else who doesn't believe what we believe. That tells you everything about humanity, its intolerance and stupidity; yes, we're all stupid to think God is better than us. When are we going to learn? God is not better than us. In fact, He's less than an ant because He can't manifest Himself in physical form like an ant. I'd say an ant is equal to a blade of grass. They're both physical, both alive. Even a pebble is superior to God. It's physical right now. You can't say the same about God unless you lie to yourself. We're all good at that. We all lie, and it's a short jump from a lie to imagination.

God is the greatest invention in the world, I'll give you that, but I'll tell you right now: He's no better than us. He's a starting point to something greater, and what is that? What could be better than God, you ask? I'll tell you, we are better than God, always have been, always will be, and if you don't believe that, you don't believe in yourself. You don't believe that you can do anything, everything; the omnipotence we attribute to God is really our omnipotence. Let's take God off His pedestal; let's put you on the pedestal instead. You can do everything; God can't do anything. He can't even feed a hungry child. You can. So, if you want to say God is inside you, okay, that's good enough for me, close enough to the truth. I'm not going to obsess about what truth is or isn't. All I'll say is, God or what have you, inside you is close enough to the truth, good enough for this world. We're good enough for this world, this imperfect world. God isn't. He's not good enough for this world; if He were, He'd be walking down the street, but He isn't–go ahead, put God on a pedestal, whatever you want to do, I don't care anymore. If you want to be wrong, I don't care, just don't kill me for saying God is less complete than an ant, just don't kill me for saying what you know to be true, that you can see an ant, you can't see God, however great He is–sure, He's the greatest of all time, but so are you, buddy, so are you.

# 48

## If I Were an Animal, I'd Have a Better Idea of Who I Am

I don't know anything about myself, I guess; I just don't. How can I know anything about myself? There's no guide to knowing yourself. Maybe I don't know the first thing about myself, and if I do know anything about myself, I could be wrong. What am I supposed to do, therefore? How am I supposed to live my life if I don't know anything about myself for sure? Maybe I don't. Oh well, what should I do? Should I just pretend I know the first thing about myself when I really don't? Should I just go through life pretending to be whoever I really am? Who am I? I don't know. I guess I'll just pretend I'm me when, really, I could be anybody. I could be anybody else walking down the street. What differentiates me from everybody else? I don't know for sure. I don't know anything for sure. All I know is I have to do something. I can't just sit here; I have to act. I have to pretend to be me and act, do something, and meet the whole world's expectations. That's what life is all about, I guess. Do something and meet all the expectations, appear to be somebody, myself for instance, when I have no idea for sure who or what I am.

I guess I'm a human being. I look like all the other human beings, though maybe I'm not. Maybe I'm an animal instead. I feel like an animal, frankly. I don't feel like a human usually. Usually, I feel like some cross between a human and an animal. Which animal? I don't know. I don't know anything about anything. All I can say is if I were an animal, I'd have a better idea of who I am. I believe animals know exactly who they are, every one of them, whether fly or giraffe. They know exactly who and what they are; there's no doubt, whereas I have a lot of doubt about who or what I'm supposed to be. People say I'm supposed to be a human being, but what do they know? Maybe I'm not supposed to be a human; maybe I'm supposed to be an animal, any animal. Maybe I really am an animal inside; maybe I'm not a human after all; maybe I'm an animal instead, and I just look like a human. It's possible that I'm an animal and not a human. I feel like an animal most of the time; I don't feel like a human much. Maybe I'm only partly human; maybe I'm mostly animal.

What if it turned out that I really was an animal and not a human? What if all the scientists took a close look at me and concluded that, despite looking like a human, I really was an animal? What would I do then? I don't know. Should I continue living like a human, or should I live like an animal? I don't know. I guess I would try to live like a human despite being an animal. It's too late to learn how to be an animal when I've spent my whole life trying to be a human. I don't know what I am, human or animal. I'm confused now; I don't know what to do. I guess I'll keep on learning; whether I'm human or animal, I'll keep on learning; that's the best I can do. I'd rather be an animal, I've decided; I decided just now. I decided I'll be an animal, even though I look like a human. I'll be an animal in human clothing. I'm going to be an animal from now on. I've always been an animal, even though I've always looked like a human. I'm some kind of freak who is really an animal but looks like any other human. I've got it all figured out now; I'm an animal–freak of nature, human-looking but animal through and through. I'm happy with that; I'm happy now. I've decided who and what I am and always have been–an animal, any kind of animal, but human-looking. I'll go through life being an animal but behaving like a human being sometimes when I have to, but otherwise, I'll behave exactly like the animal I am. I'm an animal.

# 49

## A Superior Being of The Superior Species

The world isn't worth worrying about; why worry about anything, least of all the world? It's all going to disintegrate in a billion years or so anyway, maybe two billion years; who cares? We won't be around anyway. Not even our most distant generations of human-like ancestors will be around. In fact, we'll be lucky if anything remotely resembling human beings will be around in two or three billion years. So, who cares about anything now? Why bother doing anything? Why bother getting up in the morning? I guess I should get up anyway; why not? Why not put one foot in front of the other for another day or so? It can't hurt. I didn't have anything planned anyway. I never plan anything; why bother? I just live minute-to-minute; who cares? I don't even plan what to write when I do bother writing, which isn't often. I don't have anything to say, really; why bother? It isn't going to change anything; it isn't going to save the world. So why bother writing or doing anything? I might as well just turn off my mind; there's no use thinking about anything; it isn't going to change anything or save the planet; it's too late; it's doomed; it isn't going to last another billion years, not for us humans. We're killing the planet and everything in it, so what? And even if we decided to change, to save the planet, it's all going to burn up and blow apart in two or three billion years anyway. So why bother? Why make life so much better for us even now? It's all pointless; we're not going to live forever. So why bother doing anything? Why bother learning anything when all our knowledge isn't going to save us? Why not be stupid instead? We might learn something in the process; we might learn there's something more important than knowledge and experience. What's that? I don't know, don't care. All I can say is there's nothing wrong with just sitting back and watching the world go by. Why engage? Why not just sit back and watch the trees grow? It's better than destroying the trees and everything else in the world. Why do we have to destroy everything? It's not progress; it's regress. The trees must then grow back either now or a million years from now. We're not even going to last that long; we humans who destroy everything, including our own home, Earth. Who cares?

We're not so great, we humans. We think we're the superior species, but the fact is there's another species that's better than us. Better than all other species, too. And what species is that? I don't know, don't care. All I can say is there's another species we can't even see; it's there all around us. We can't see them, but they're there all around us. What am I talking about? Am I high? All I can say is they're better than us in every way. They're kind of like us, except better. They're kind of like angels but better. In fact, they're the superior species not only on Earth but on every habitable planet. There's plenty of them. These superior beings fly all over the place, all over the universe, in fact. Don't take my word for it; just look around; you'll see superior beings flying all over the place. You just have to be able to see them. I see them; I've always seen them. They're not just in my imagination, though they're in my imagination too. They're both real and unreal. What am I talking about?

135

Am I high? All I know is they're all over the place. They're in Heaven; they're in Hell; they're on Earth and on every habitable planet in the universe. I know because I've been on every habitable planet in the universe, in a sense. If you've been on one habitable planet, you've been on them all. But really, I have been on every planet; I physically went there. In fact, I'm on them all right now. I can be on every habitable planet all at the same time. How is that possible?

It's because I'm one of those superior beings of the superior species. They're kind of like humans, except better in every way. I should know because I'm both human and a superior being, kind of like God, except better in every way. That's what these superior beings are like. They're better than man, better than God, better than the Devil. In fact, these better beings are all man and God and the Devil all combined into one superior being. That's just the way it is; that's the destiny of the world and of the entire universe, too. All these superior beings are going to be flying all over the place, across the universe, back and forth, because there's nothing better to do when you're of the superior species. You've already conquered the entire universe. So why not just fly around and do whatever you want? There's no destiny, no purpose, just be superior in every way. That's what these beings are. Superior just like us humans, except better, smarter. We could be like them if we wanted. We could be them if we wanted; we just don't want to. We don't want to be superior; we're happy just the way we are. But that doesn't change that there are superior, flying beings all over the place like insects, except better than us humans. Yes, insects and flying beings are all over the universe, and they're better than us humans, always have been and always will be. These superior beings or insects they're all the same; they fly like insects, they fly like superior beings, except they're human too. They're both human and superior beings all at the same time; they're like God except better, like man except better, like insects except better. They're everything there ever was or will be; they're like the universe itself except better; they're beyond the universe; they're in a different realm above Heaven and below Hell. They're on Earth, in other words. They're particles and the universe itself; they're everything and nothing both. They're everything you can imagine, and you can imagine everything and beyond if you're a superior being. That's all it takes to be a superior being of the superior species: just imagine everything and beyond.

# 50

# I Was God for A Second

I make everything up as I walk along, with no destination, no ambition, homeless, with no plans, no agenda, no reality. I'm more interested in what isn't here. What am I talking about? I don't care, and I don't know; I just sit here on the curb, watching people and cars go by, not people-watching per se but just hoping to see someone who is really alive; I mean living not in reality but living in nonreality. How do they do that? How do they live in nonreality when reality is all around and consuming them as if they were food? As if all we are is food for reality, as if reality is more important than we are, and all we can do is be eaten by it, as if we're not important, as if reality is the most important thing in the universe. I personally don't want to be eaten up by reality; I'd rather ignore reality and live in a dream world where I can sit on a curb, worry about nothing, not have to pay attention to what everyone else is doing and do the same; where I do whatever I want, even if I don't want to do anything, just sit here and figure it all out–what life means, if anything. I want to figure it all out before I take one step toward doing anything. Why do anything if I don't have it all figured out yet? Even if it means sitting here a lifetime and doing nothing, if I don't have it all figured out yet–what I should do with my life, if anything.

Who says I have to do anything with my life? Who says I have to do anything at all? Why not just be a so-called failure? Why not be a so-called parasite, living off other people who are just drones anyway? I don't want to be a drone like them. I'd rather be a parasite than a drone. Drones have no brains, let alone souls. I'd rather sit here on this curb for a whole lifetime, trying to figure out what a soul is. I don't know, but I'll sit here as long as it takes to figure out what a soul is. Who knows? All I know is it's important, more important than living itself. Or maybe the soul is life itself. Who knows? I don't, don't really want to know, just want to feel whatever is true; don't have to know what is true, just have to feel whatever is true. The only thing I know for sure at this point is that feeling is what it's all about: life. Knowing comes second, if at all. Who knows? I don't and don't want to know; I just want to feel the whole universe. That's the most important thing in the whole universe: to feel everything.

What do I mean by feeling everything? Don't I know I have to earn a living? Who cares about feeling everything, or even anything at all, if I haven't figured out how to earn a living? As if living matters. It doesn't matter to me. I'm serious; living doesn't mean much to me. I could die tomorrow or even today, and it wouldn't mean a lot to me. Nothing means a lot to me. All that matters to me is feeling everything. What do I mean by feeling everything? I mean feeling every little thing; every little speck of dust; I want to feel it as it floats through the air. That means I have to be everywhere if I am to feel every little speck of dust in the universe. It means I have to be all over the universe, all at the same time. That's impossible for humans or for most humans. I can do it, though; I can be all over the entire universe, all at the same time. How is that possible? It is; that's all I know. I don't want to know anything other than

139

how to be all over the entire universe at the same time. Who can do that? Me, and only me. It's true because yesterday, I was all over the entire universe for a second–just a second–and no one else was there, only me. A dog was there to keep me company, but there were no other humans. What does that mean? Nothing, as far as I'm concerned. I was the only one who was all over the whole universe at the same time; no other humans, only a dog, was with me, keeping me company. Who knows whether the dog was there first, all over the universe, or if I was there first? It doesn't matter who was there first. All that matters is we were there together, the dog and me. I don't know whose dog it was; maybe it was my dog for a second. I was only there for a second all over the universe, and then I came back to reality.

I was in heaven for a mere second, but it felt like a lifetime, being in heaven. I guess it was heaven. People call it heaven, but it felt to me like it was the entire universe that I was in. You can call it heaven if you want. I don't care. I don't care about anything except getting back to heaven or the entire universe. I'll sit here on this curb until I figure out how to get back there, heaven, the entire universe. You can call me a loser, a parasite. I don't care. All I know is I was in heaven for a second yesterday, and I'll sit here on this curb until I figure it all out–the meaning of the universe, life. That's all that's important: getting back to heaven or whatever it is. Who cares what it is? All I know is I want to get back there, because that's where all the meaning is, heaven, nowhere else. There's no meaning here on earth except figuring out how to get back to the universe, heaven. That's all that matters, at least to me. You do what you want, and maybe you'll get to the universe, or heaven, or whatever you want to call it. I don't want to call it anything. I don't want to call anything anything. I just want to be there, heaven or whatever.

Maybe I'm there right now, sitting on this curb. Maybe I'm in heaven or on the opposite side of the universe right now, sitting on this dirty curb, this dirty sidewalk. Maybe heaven is right here. I think it is. I don't know for sure. I don't know anything for sure, don't want to know anything for sure. All I want is to feel everything for sure. That's possible when I'm in heaven. I was there yesterday for a second, and in that second, I felt everything for sure. I had no doubt about anything, least of all myself. In that second, I had absolute confidence in myself as God. That's right, I was God for a second yesterday, and today, I'm going to spend all day sitting here on this dirty sidewalk until I figure it all out: how to get back to heaven or wherever I was yesterday for a second. I don't know how I got there for a second, but I got there. Maybe I got there by sitting on this same dirty sidewalk, figuring it all out, homeless, starving, nothing to my name. Maybe I got to heaven yesterday for a second by having nothing, wanting nothing, being nothing, not even a respectable member of the human race. I was an outcast, but I made it to heaven yesterday for a second. That's good enough for me, heaven for a second. Maybe today, I can get back there for a second. All I know is I'll sit here in the dirt, until I figure it all out, the meaning of the universe. The answer is all in my head, even though I know nothing, I never learned anything in school. Maybe I'll figure it all out anyway. I did yesterday, so I can do it again today and get to heaven for a second. That's all I need to keep me going, getting to heaven for a second today. I don't

141

need food or anything else today; I just need to get back to heaven again, as I was yesterday and as I was on the day I was born. I think I was in heaven on the day I was born. Maybe I was just part of the universe on that day. Maybe I was just the universe on the day I was born.

I want to be the universe again, and I'll sit here on the curb until I get back to the universe, heaven, even for a second. I'll give up everything to get back there for a mere second. That's why I have nothing, so I can get back to heaven, the universe, earth, the dirty ground, the dirty curb; a mere parasite, but in heaven for a second every day. All I need is to be in heaven for a second every day. I'll give up everything for that. I've already given up everything for heaven. I'll do it again today. I'll be in heaven today, me and that dog.

# About the Author

Mo Pulido has a B.A. in English Language and Literature from the University of Michigan. He lives in Arlington, Virginia.